Our Story

Back in 1984, we were next-door neighbors raising our families in the little town of Delaware, Ohio. We were two moms with small children looking for a way to do what we loved and stay home with the kids too. We shared a love of home cooking and making memories with family & friends. After many a conversation over the backyard fence, Gooseberry Patch was born.

We put together the first catalog & cookbooks at our kitchen tables and packed boxes from the basement, enlisting the help of our loved ones wherever we could. From that little family, we've grown to include an amazing group of creative folks who love cooking, decorating and creating as much as we do.

Hard to believe it's been over 25 years since those kitchen-table days. Today, we're best known for our homestyle, family-friendly cookbooks. We love hand-picking the recipes and are tickled to share our inspiration, ideas and more with you! One thing's for sure, we couldn't have done it without our friends all across the country. Whether you've been along for the ride from the beginning or are just discovering us, welcome to our family!

Your friends at Gooseberry Patch

Find us here too!

Join our **Circle of Friends** and discover free recipes & crafts, plus giveaways & more! Visit our website or blog to join and be sure to follow us on Facebook & Twitter too.

Join our Circle of Friends

VIDEOS

Find us on Facebook

Read Our Blog

Follow us on twitter

www.gooseberrypatch.com

OH. SO. FESTIVE Felt

Cheery sights of the season are even better when they're simple to create. Felt ornaments and a floral skirt trim the tree in happy colors. Needle-Felted Stockings brighten the hallway or mantel, while the Felted Ball Garland is quick to make with wool roving and foam balls. Easy-stitch presents like a gift card holder or scarf will be welcomed by everyone. If the kids want to get involved, they can help you make a Felted Ball Centerpiece, Dangling Ornaments and Ski Pals. This felted Christmas is so much fun to fashion!

Loopy Ornaments, Snowflower Ornaments and Felt Tree Topper instructions begin on page 112.

Loopy Ornament   Snowflower Ornament   Felt Tree Topper

Christmas

Book 12

Content and Artwork by
Gooseberry Patch Company

LEISURE ARTS

Editor-in-Chief: Susan White Sullivan
Designer Relations Director: Debra Nettles
Craft Publications Director: Cheryl Johnson
Art Publications Director: Rhonda Shelby
Special Projects Director: Susan Frantz Wiles
Senior Prepress Director: Mark Hawkins

EDITORIAL STAFF

TECHNICAL

Technical Writer: Laura Siar Bertram
Technical Associates: Sarah J. Green, Mary Sullivan Hutcheson and Lois J. Long
Licensed Product Coordinator: Jean Lewis

EDITORIAL

Editorial Writer: Susan McManus Johnson

FOODS

Foods Editor: Jane Kenner Prather
Contributing Test Kitchen Staff: Rose Glass Klein

DESIGN

Design Captain: Becky Werle
Designers: Kim Hamblin, Anne Pulliam Stocks and Lori Wenger

ART

Art Category Manager: Lora Puls
Lead Graphic Artist: Angela Ormsby Stark
Graphic Artists: Jacob Casleton, Amy Temple and Janie Marie Wright
Imaging Technicians: Brian Hall, Stephanie Johnson and Mark R. Potter
Photography Manager: Katherine Laughlin
Contributing Photo Stylist: Christy Myers
Publishing Systems Administrator: Becky Riddle
Publishing Systems Assistants: Clint Hanson and John Rose

BUSINESS STAFF

Vice President and Chief Operations Officer: Tom Siebenmorgen
Director of Finance and Administration: Laticia Mull Dittrich
Vice President, Sales and Marketing: Pam Stebbins
National Accounts Director: Martha Adams
Sales and Services Director: Margaret Reinold
Information Technology Director: Hermine Linz
Controller: Francis Caple
Vice President, Operations: Jim Dittrich
Comptroller, Operations: Rob Thieme
Retail Customer Service Manager: Stan Raynor
Print Production Manager: Fred F. Pruss

OXMOOR HOUSE

Vice President, Publishing Director: Jim Childs
Editorial Director: Susan Payne Dobbs
Brand Manager: Terri Laschober Robertson
Senior Editor: Rebecca Brennan
Foods Editor: Kelly Hooper Troiano
Production Manager: Terri Beste-Farley
Photography Director: Jim Bathie
Senior Photo Stylist: Kay E. Clarke
Associate Photo Stylist: Katherine Eckert Coyne
Test Kitchens Director: Elizabeth Tyler Austin
Test Kitchens Assistant Director: Julie Christopher
Test Kitchens Professionals: Allison E. Cox, Julie Gunter, Kathleen Royal Phillips, Catherine Crowell Steele and Ashley T. Strickland
Contributing Food Stylists: Margaret Dickey, Alyson Haynes and Ana Price Kelly
Contributing Photographer: Lee Harrelson
Contributing Photo Stylist: Mindy Shapiro

Library of Congress Control Number: 2009937171
Hardcover ISBN-10: 0-8487-3323-1
Softcover ISBN-10: 0-8487-3324-X
Hardcover ISBN-13: 978-0-8487-3323-0
Softcover ISBN-13: 978-0-8487-3324-7

10 9 8 7 6 5 4 3 2 1

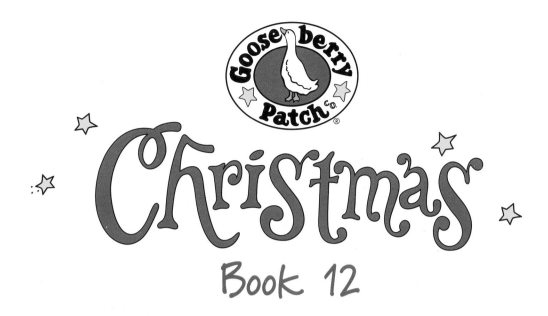

Christmas
Book 12

Christmas

Gooseberry Patch

Sending warm & cozy Christmas wishes
to all our family & friends!

Pretty little flowers bloom on the Needle-Felted Tree Skirt, and you won't believe how simple it is to make a Felted Ball Garland or Dangling Ornament.

Needle-Felted Tree Skirt

- 41" square of red wool felt
- string
- water-soluble fabric marker
- thumbtack
- tracing paper
- ½ yard of 36"w burgundy wool felt
- green, ivory and rose wool felt
- scallop-edged scissors and pinking shears
- red dotted fabric
- green wool yarn
- needle felting tool and mat
- 2-hole and shank buttons
- fabric glue

1. For the skirt, follow *Making a Fabric Circle* (page 138) and use a 20" string measurement to mark the outer cutting line on the red wool felt. Remove the tack and use a 1" string measurement to mark the inner cutting line.

2. Cut through all felt layers along the drawn lines. Unfold the circle. Cut a back opening from the outer edge to the center opening.

3. Use the patterns on page 146 and cut 5 sets of felt flowers and leaves, scalloping the round flower edges. Cut 36 felt semi-circles for the border. Pinking the edges, cut 10 fabric flower centers and 10 smaller felt centers; set aside.

4. Pin 5 groupings of flowers and leaves on the skirt, about 2" from the outer edge (we varied the arrangements just for fun). Pin a 12" yarn "stem" to each tulip.

5. Follow *Needle Felting* (page 140) to apply the stems, flowers and leaves to the skirt. Sew the flower centers and buttons in place.

6. For the border, arrange, then glue the semi-circles along the outer edge of the skirt.

Needle-Felted Tree Skirt

Felted Ball Garland

Felted Ball Garland
- plastic basin
- liquid dishwashing detergent (without scents or dyes)
- shades of green, red and ivory wool roving
- foam balls (we used 1", 1¹/₂" and 2" dia. balls)
- rubber gloves (optional)
- yarn needle
- yarn

The whole family will have a ball making this garland! Follow *Felted Wool Balls* (page 140) to cover foam balls with roving. String the balls on yarn to form a garland...if you like, make graduated garland lengths to fit around the tree.

Dangling Ornaments
Instructions are on page 113.

SEEDLINGS

Dangling Ornament

Felted Ball Wreath

Wool roving adds its merry hues to foam balls on the easy Felted Ball Wreath. On the Needle-Felted Stockings, a felting tool punches the fibers of the same colorful wool into felt fabric.

Felted Ball Wreath

- plastic basin
- liquid dishwashing detergent (without scents or dyes)
- shades of green, red, ivory, blue and rust wool roving
- foam balls (we used 13 each of 1¹/₂", 2" and 2¹/₂" dia. balls)
- rubber gloves (optional)
- embroidery floss
- large-eye needle
- 12" dia. wire wreath form (ours has 4 wire rings)
- hot glue gun
- 1¹/₂ yards of 1¹/₂"w grosgrain ribbon
- plastic ring or aluminum can pull tab

1. Follow *Felted Wool Balls* (page 140) to cover foam balls with roving.

(continued on page 113)

Needle-Felted Stockings

Create festive stockings with wool roving and felt in colors you love!

Green Stocking
- ¹/₃ yard of green wool felt
- scallop-edged scissors
- cream wool felt
- pinking shears
- fabric scraps
- plastic basin

- liquid dishwashing detergent (without scents or dyes)
- red and ivory wool roving
- two 1" dia. foam balls
- rubber gloves (optional)
- craft knife and cutting mat
- yarn needle
- red yarn
- hot glue gun
- needle felting tool and mat

1. Enlarge the pattern on page 145 to 200%. Use the pattern and cut 2 green felt stocking pieces. Use scallop-edged scissors to cut four 2³/₄" diameter cream felt circles. Use pinking shears to cut four 1³/₄" fabric circles.

(continued on page 114)

Ski Pals are sweet little sit-abouts that inspire smiles all season. To add color to a table, make a quick Felted Ball Centerpiece.

Anything is Possible!

Ski Pals

- acrylic paints
- paintbrushes
- 4½" craft sticks (for skis)
- wood doll pins with flat bottoms
- 1¼" dia. wood doll heads with ⅝" holes
- hot glue gun
- ribbon scraps
- embroidery floss
- tracing paper
- wool felt scraps
- 10mm pom-poms
- chenille stems
- 3½" flat wood sandwich picks or slim craft sticks (for ski poles)

1. For each skier, paint 2 skis, a doll pin body and a head. Add face and "button" details.
2. Glue the head on the body and a ribbon "belt" around the waist. Glue floss lengths to the head for bangs. For the girl, braid six 7" floss lengths and knot the ends; glue the center of the braid to the top of her head.
3. Using the pattern on page 144, cut a wool felt hat. Glue the front to the top of the head. Glue the back edges together and add the pom-pom.
4. Glue chenille stem arms at the back of the doll pin. Glue on the skis and ski poles, making sure the poles touch the ground for added support.

Ski Pals

Felted Ball Centerpiece

Felted Ball Centerpiece

For an eye-catching arrangement, follow *Felted Wool Balls* (page 140) to cover foam balls with wool roving. Fill a rustic bowl with balls of all different sizes and a variety of cozy colors.

Fanciful Journal Cover

- cream felt
- purchased journal (ours is 5"x7")
- tissue paper
- assorted felt and fabric scraps
- embroidery floss
- water-soluble fabric marker
- cotton swab
- buttons and beads

Read Embroidery Stitches on page 139 before beginning. Use 3 strands of floss.

1. For the cover, cut a cream felt rectangle ¹/₂" larger than the open journal on all sides. Cut 2 inside pocket rectangles the same height as the cover and ¹/₂" narrower than the journal front.
2. Use the patterns on page 146, or cut freeform flowers and leaves from felt and fabric (we cut around a floral motif for one flower). Arrange and pin the shapes on the front cover. Sew the shapes to the cover with freeform stitching lines.
3. Use the *Tissue Paper Method* (page 138) and the embroidery pattern on page 146 to work a *Lazy Daisy* and *French Knot* flower.
4. Draw swirling stems and leaves with the marker. Sew over each line several times. Remove any marker lines with a damp cotton swab. Sew freeform lines around the edges of the cover. Add buttons and beads to flower centers.
5. Match wrong sides and use a ¹/₄" seam allowance to sew a pocket rectangle along the outer edges of the cover at each end; insert the journal.

Fanciful Journal Cover

Sweet Gift Card Holder

- tracing paper
- felt scraps for bird and leaves
- felted wool scraps for wing and holder
- embroidery floss
- hook and loop fastener
- fabric glue
- 14" length of ¹/₄"w ribbon
- 2 small wood beads
- alphabet beads

Adjust the size of the holder as you wish (our card is 3³/₈"x2¹/₈").

(continued on page 113)

Sweet Gift Card Holder

Appliqués, beads and embroidery stitches bring the Fanciful Journal Cover and Sweet Gift Card Holder to life with whimsical designs. For the gal who has everything, why not create a blooming Cell Phone Cozy with a 3-D flower?

Cell Phone Cozy

Cell Phone Cozy
- blue wool felt
- water-soluble fabric marker
- assorted felt and fabric scraps
- pinking shears
- cotton swab
- decorative scrapbook brads
- red wool roving
- needle felting tool and mat
- jumbo rickrack
- swivel clasp

Adjust the felt size as needed to fit your phone (the finished size of our cozy is 3¼"x5½"). Use a ¼" seam allowance for all sewing.

(continued on page 114)

Woolly Pincushions

Make pincushions for friends who love to sew.

Green Pincushion

- plastic basin
- liquid dishwashing detergent (without scents or dyes)
- green and red wool roving
- 1" and 3" dia. foam balls
- rubber gloves (optional)
- red felt
- needle felting tool
- red embroidery floss
- long sharp needle
- hot glue gun
- tin gelatin mold

1. Follow *Felted Wool Balls* (page 140) to cover the foam balls with green roving. Cut a dozen 2" diameter red felt circles; set aside.
2. Follow *Needle Felting* (page 140) and use red roving to apply dots to the large ball.

(continued on page 115)

Felted Flower Pln

Woolly Pincushions

Make these day-brightening gifts for all your friends! If you know someone who sews, treat her to one of three Woolly Pincushions. The Felted Flower Pin and Felted Scarf are pretty presents that are actually made from worn sweaters!

Felted Flower Pin
- worn wool sweater (with at least 60% wool content)
- tracing paper
- beading needle and thread
- seed beads
- hot glue gun
- pin back

1. Follow *Felting* (page 140) to felt the sweater.
2. Use the pattern on page 144 and cut 8 petals from the felted sweater. Pinching each petal at the point, sew the points together to form a flower; pull tight and knot the thread ends.
3. Add seed beads and hot glue the pin back to the back of the flower.

A HAT ON EVERY HEAD... ...A MITTEN ON EVERY HAND.

Felted Scarf

Felted Scarf
- 2-color worn wool sweater or 2 different-colored sweaters (with at least 60% wool content)
- rotary cutter, ruler and mat
- seam ripper

This warm & toasty scarf is designed to be worn with the seam allowances showing for added texture. Match wrong sides and use a ¼" seam allowance for all sewing.

1. Follow *Felting* (page 140) to felt the sweater.
2. Cut 20 strips from the sweater (six 9"x1½" and four 6"x1½" strips from each color).
3. Matching long edges and alternating colors, sew 4 same-size strips together. Repeat to sew the remaining strips together in sets of 4.

4. Matching short ends, sew the 9"-long panels together. Use the seam ripper to make a 2" opening in the center of one of the 9" end panels. Sew across the ends of the opening to secure. Sew a 6" panel to each end panel.
5. Baste across each end of the scarf. Pull to gather; knot the ends.
6. To wear, thread one scarf end through the opening on the opposite end.

the Twelve Days of Christmas

For a Christmas theme that will have everyone singing along, set the table with sweetly stitched items from The Twelve Days of Christmas. Pear Place Cards and Partridge Napkin Rings welcome each guest, while Chair-back Swags celebrate the season with vintage style. In the middle of it all, a pear tree centerpiece blooms with embroidered ornaments. The Country Friends have also whipped up a half-dozen aprons you and your kitchen helpers can enjoy all year!

Chair-back Swags instructions are on page 115.

Chair-back Swags

The branches of the 12 Days Centerpiece tree are simply sections cut from wood embroidery hoops! Framed in small painted hoops, the ornaments feature easy embroidery and fabric appliqués for extra color.

12 Days Centerpiece

12 Days Centerpiece
12 Days Ornaments
- paper-backed fusible web
- fabric scraps for appliqués (we used 6 different fabrics)
- tissue paper
- water-soluble fabric marker
- twelve 6" squares of white duck cloth or heavyweight cotton
- embroidery floss
- teal acrylic paint
- paintbrush
- twelve 3" dia. wood embroidery hoops
- sandpaper
- 8" length of $1/8$"w silk ribbon

Read Embroidery Stitches on page 139 before beginning. Use 2 strands of floss.

1. Fuse web to the back of each fabric scrap.
2. Follow the *Water-Soluble Fabric Marker Method* (page 138) and transfer the patterns on page 148 onto duck cloth squares. Using the photos and patterns, cut fabric scrap appliqués. Fuse the appliqués in place.
3. Embroider the designs using *Stem Stitch, French Knot* and *Lazy Daisy* stitches.
4. Paint the hoops teal; then, sand for an aged appearance. Insert the stitched pieces in the hoops; trim excess fabric. Sew a silk ribbon bow to the 5 Golden Rings design.

Pear Tree

- transfer paper
- 18"x24" piece of 3/16" thick foam core
- craft knife and cutting mat
- small hand saw
- 8", 12", 18" and 23" dia. wood embroidery hoops
  (we used one ring from each)
- sandpaper
- green acrylic paint
- paintbrush
- hot glue gun
- 5 yards of 3/8"w ribbon, cut into 15" lengths
- 12 Days Ornaments
- tracing paper
- cardstock
- green felt

The 12 Days of Christmas adorn this cheery tree made with embroidery hoop branches.

1. Enlarge the pear tree and base patterns on page 149 to 249%. Transfer the patterns to foam core; cut out with the craft knife.
2. For the branches, use the saw to cut a 5" length from the 8" hoop. Cut a 10", 15" and 20" length from each larger hoop. Sand the edges.
3. Paint the tree, base and branches green on all sides. Slide the tree onto the base at the slits. Sand the branch edges for an aged appearance.
4. Center and securely hot glue the largest branch on the tree, resting it on the top of the base. Glue each of the remaining branches to the tree 4" apart.
5. Cut 2 slits through the center of the tree just above and below the second branch from the top. Thread a ribbon length through the slits from the back of the tree and tie the 5 Golden Rings hoop to the front. Tie a bow to the Partridge hoop and rest the hoop on top of the tree. Tie each remaining hoop to a branch with ribbon.
6. Using the patterns on page 149, cut cardstock tags and felt leaves. Sew a tag to each bow and hot glue the leaves to the branches.

When guests see the perky Partridge Napkin Rings, they'll know you're wishing them a very merry Christmas, indeed! The napkins are precut fat quarters (fabric pieces cut approx. 18"x22"), hemmed to prevent raveling. The Pear Place Cards double as festive favors, and are so pleasant to sew!

Partridge Napkin Rings

- tracing paper
- fabric scraps
- teal, dark teal and peach felt
- fabric glue
- pearl stamens (from a craft store wedding section)
- embroidery floss
- black E beads for eyes

Read Embroidery Stitches on page 139 before beginning. Use 2 strands of floss.

1. For each napkin ring, use the patterns on page 147 and cut one wing from fabric. Cut 2 partridges and one tail, breast and beak from felt. Cut a 1⁷⁄₈"x5¼" felt band.
2. Glue the tail, breast and wing to one bird. Glue the birds together, tucking 3 stamens between the layers at the head. Work Blanket Stitches around the bird and Running Stitches near the wing edges. Sew the bead and glue the beak in place.
3. Overlap and glue or sew the ends of the felt band together; glue to the back of the partridge.

Partridge Napkin Rings

Pear Place Cards

Pear Place Cards

- scraps of 4 print fabrics
- green and brown felt scraps
- polyester fiberfill
- water-soluble fabric marker or white colored pencil
- embroidery floss
- upholstery needle
- 1" dia. buttons

Match right sides and use a 1/4" seam allowance for all sewing unless otherwise noted.

1. For each place card, enlarge the patterns on page 147 to 200%. Using the patterns, cut 4 pear pieces from fabrics; cut 2 leaves and one stem from felt.

2. Sew 2 pear pieces together along one long edge, stopping 1/2" from the bottom point. Continue to sew all 4 pieces together. Clip the curves and turn right side out. Stuff the pear and sew the bottom opening closed.

3. Write a name on one leaf. Using 3 strands of floss, work *Stem Stitch* (page 139) letters; then, layer and join the leaves with *Blanket Stitches*.

4. Fold the bottom of the stem up 1/4". Using 6 strands of floss and the upholstery needle, sew through the fold and the base of the leaf. Run the needle down through the stem, pear and a button. Run the needle back through the button and pull tight to tuft. Thread the needle through the button a few more times, catch the fabric and knot the thread ends.

Pleated Half Apron
Pocketed Half Apron
Instructions begin on page 115.

Ruffled Half Apron
- 18"x18" vintage-look fabric piece
- ½ yard of 60"w vintage-look fabric for ruffle and waistband/ties
- 1⅛" dia. self-covered button
- fabric scrap
- ½"w and 1"w grosgrain ribbons
- liquid fray preventative

Match right sides and use a ½" seam allowance for all sewing unless otherwise noted. This apron rests below the waist. If you wish, cut patterns from paper first and adjust the height or width of the pieces (and yardage) as needed to fit.

If you have a vintage tablecloth that's been stained or torn, use the good section to make an apron. That's how the Country Friends added three of these colorful creations to the Christmas countdown. For the rest, they used new fabric with an old-fashioned look. What better way to celebrate the Twelve Days than with six bakers baking?

1. Cut the fabric square in half diagonally; set aside one piece for another use. Cut a 7"x56" ruffle and a 3½"x88" waistband/tie strip (this will need to be pieced).
2. Press one long edge of the ruffle ¼" to the wrong side twice; hem. Baste along the long raw edge of the ruffle. Matching raw edges, gather and pin the ruffle to fit the short sides of the fabric triangle; knot the thread ends. Sew the ruffle to the triangle; press the seam allowances toward the triangle.
3. Center and pin, then sew the waistband/tie strip along the raw edge of the ruffled triangle skirt. Matching right sides and long raw edges, fold the strip in half. If you like, trim the tie ends to a point. Leaving the ruffled skirt and waistband unstitched, sew along the long edges and short ends of the ties. Clip the corners, turn right side out and press, turning the raw edges of the waistband under; topstitch.
4. Cover the button with fabric. Sew the button and layered ribbon bows to the waistband. Apply fray preventative to the ribbon ends.

Ruffled Half Apron
Pleated Half Apron
Pocketed Half Apron

Red-Trimmed Bib Apron
Full Cinched Apron
Green-Trimmed Bib Apron
Instructions begin on page 116.

Red-Trimmed Bib Apron
Full Cinched Apron
Green-Trimmed Bib Apron

Woodsy Welcome

Nature lovers will enjoy the refreshing simplicity of this woodland holiday theme! Feed the neighborhood birds with a Feathered Friends' Wreath or Hanging Log Feeder. Make bird-friendly ornaments for a tree in your yard. Light up your porch with birch-bark or green apple candles; then settle on an Inviting Bench to watch the little creatures enjoy the treats you've provided. The Yuletide is a perfect time to enjoy the beauty of nature, and it's so easy to do!

Natural Wreath instructions are on page 118.

Natural Wreath

Visitors will feel at home when they see a cozy Woodsy Welcome sign near your door. Make your porch or entryway warm and inviting when you display Woodland Candles.

Woodsy Welcome

Woodsy Welcome

- transfer paper
- 10³/₄"x9" pre-rusted metal sheet
- acrylic paints
- paintbrushes
- alphabet stickers and rub-ons
- sandpaper
- clear acrylic matte sealer
- craft glue
- two ½" dia. buttons
- tack hammer
- 4 upholstery tacks
- 12"x12" wood plaque (we painted ours white and sanded the edges)
- 30" length of 1½"w ribbon
- staple gun

1. Enlarge the pattern on page 150 to 167%. Transfer the outline of the owl and branches to the metal sheet.
2. Basecoat the design; allow to dry. Transfer, then paint the details. Arrange the stickers and rub-ons for placement only; then, paint light-colored shapes as background to some of the letters. Lightly sand the sign for a weathered look.
3. Apply stickers and rub-ons to the sign. Apply sealer.
4. Glue on buttons for eyes. Use the hammer to tack the sign onto the plaque. Knot the ribbon near each end and staple to the plaque.

Bird Food Mix
(shown on page 32)
Birds will be drawn to this mixture!

$\frac{1}{4}$ c. lard or bacon grease
$\frac{1}{4}$ c. peanut butter
cornmeal to thicken (don't use a cornmeal mix with baking powder)
birdseed

Melt the lard and peanut butter in a large skillet on the stove; remove from heat. Stir in equal amounts of cornmeal and birdseed until thickened. Fill the holes in the Hanging Log Feeder (page 32) with the mixture. Refrigerate the unused portion for a few days or freeze in a covered plastic container.

Woodland Candles
Pin pieces of birch bark around pillar candles of different sizes and add raffia bows as you wish. For fresh apple candleholders, cut tea-light or votive-size holes from the tops of green apples; dip in lemon juice. Place a candle in each apple holder. Don't leave burning candles unattended…you'll want to stay and enjoy the glow!

Woodland Candles

Help the birds enjoy the season with a Hanging Log Feeder filled with Bird Food Mix. A Feathered Friends' Wreath will attract a wide variety of birds that like fruit and bread.

Bird Food Mix
Hanging Log Feeder

Feathered Friends' Wreath
- whole grain bagels
- sewing needle
- upholstery thread or dental floss
- dried plums
- dried apricots
- 16" dia. wire wreath form (ours has 4 wire rings)
- raw peanuts in their shells
- dried cranberries

Treat your favorite birds to a tasty (and colorful) wreath of their own!

1. Cut bagels into wedges; allow to dry.
2. Alternating fruit pieces, string plums and apricots on thread, wrapping the thread around the inner ring of the wreath as you go. Fill the inner ring and tie the ends together.
3. In an alternating pattern, string three peanuts, then several cranberries on thread. Repeat, wrapping the thread around the outer ring of the wreath. Fill the outer ring and tie the ends together.
4. String bagel wedges on thread, wrapping the thread around the center rings of the wreath and piercing the fruit on the other rings from time to time for stability. Fill the center rings and tie the ends together.

Bird Food Mix
Recipe is on page 31.

Hanging Log Feeder
Instructions are on page 119.

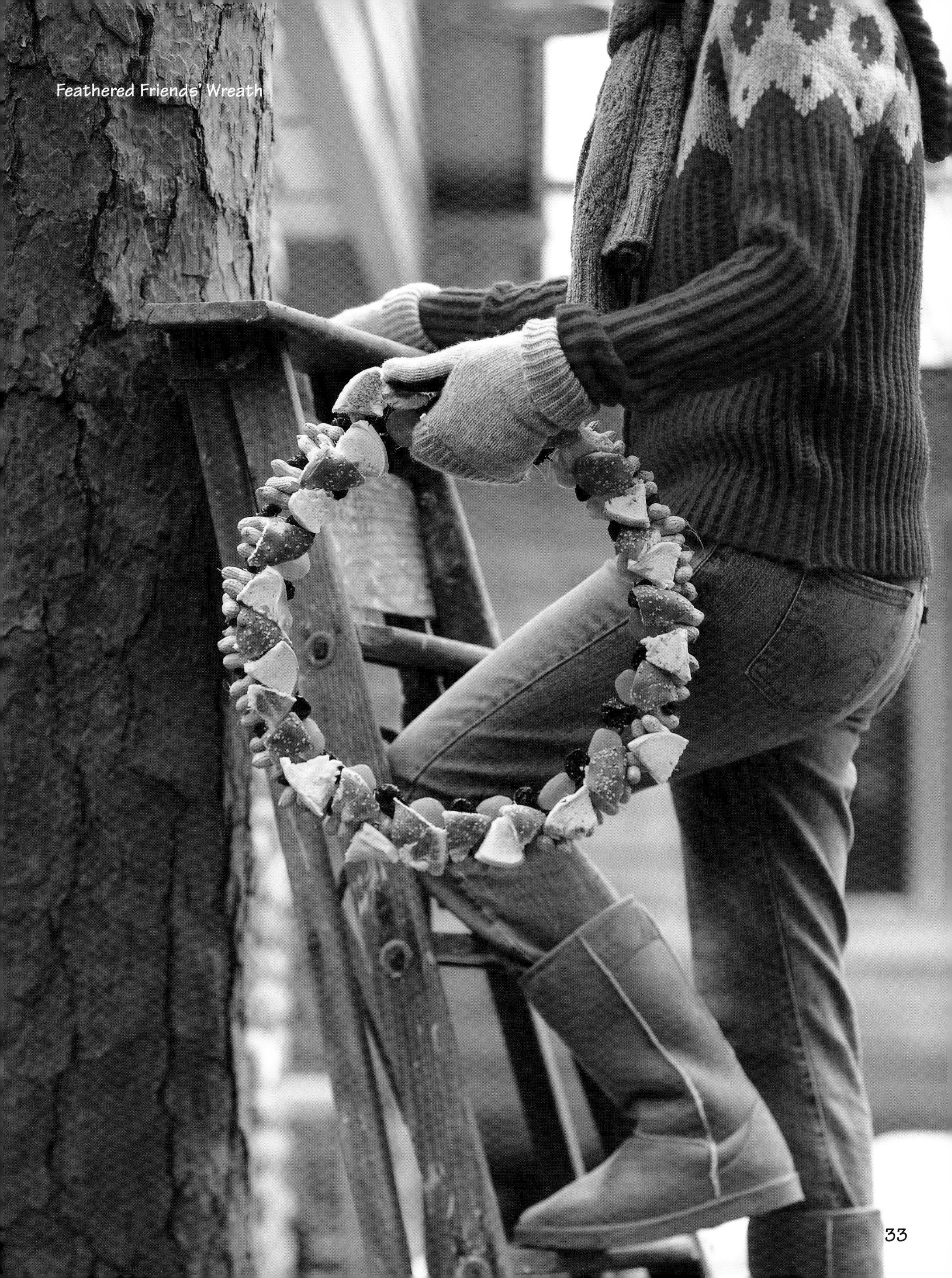

Feathered Friends' Wreath

Birdseed Stars, Birdie Icicles and Green Apple Dangles will have all your winged neighbors flitting in for a visit. The Paper Snowflakes are just for fun!

Birdseed Stars

For each star, use wood glue to adhere craft sticks in a star shape; allow to dry. Spread birdseed on wax paper. Using a disposable foam brush, apply non-toxic craft glue over the star and press into the birdseed; allow to dry. For the hanger, run jute twine through a hole drilled through the top of the star.

Birdie Icicles

These hanging ornaments will delight your feathered friends. Alternating dried bagel wedges and dried plums, use a large needle and run thin jute twine through the pieces. Knot at the bottom and tie a hanging loop at the top.

Green Apple Dangles

Cut each green apple into 8 slices; soak in lemon juice. Using 4 slices for each ornament, pierce each slice from a different angle with a large needle and run thin jute twine through the apples. Knot at the bottom and tie a hanging loop at the top.

Paper Snowflakes
- 8¹/₂"x11" parchment paper sheets
- small sharp scissors
- 1" snowflake punch
- transfer paper
- clear nylon thread
- sharp needle

Use our patterns or draw your own designs to make a flurry of unique snowflakes for your tree! Hang the flakes on the tree on dry winter days or all season long in a sheltered spot.

(continued on page 119)

Birdseed Star

Birdie Icicle

Green Apple Dangle

Paper Snowflake

BE KIND TO ALL CREATURES GREAT and SMALL

34

Log Tote

Carrying firewood is a tidy task when you use an easy-to-sew Log Tote. It's simple to paint the Inviting Bench, and the crocheted Woodland Throw will keep you warm while you enjoy the sights of nature!

Log Tote
Instructions are on page 120.

Inviting Bench

- wood bench (ours has a 1'x4' top)
- primer
- cream latex paint
- paintbrushes
- transfer paper
- acrylic paints (we used 3 shades of brown and burnt umber)
- coarse sandpaper
- clear acrylic matte sealer

1. Prime, then paint the bench cream.

2. Follow *Sizing Patterns* (page 138) to size the patterns on page 150 to fit your bench…we enlarged ours to 200%. Transfer the patterns and paint the trees. Refer to *Drybrushing* (page 138) to brush the bench with burnt umber.

3. Heavily sand the bench to give it an aged appearance. Apply sealer.

Woodland Throw

Instructions begin on page 120.

Inviting Bench
Woodland Throw

A Skater's Christmas

One of the thrills of the season is tying on skates and stepping onto the ice. With their own memories of childhood skating parties in mind, the Country Friends discovered that ice skating is a perfect theme for Christmas decorations! Little wool accessories and colorful knitting needles are oh-so cozy tucked into the branches of a wintry tree. When the Knit Scarf garland and Knit Mitten ornaments are made a little larger, they're wonderful gifts for a child! Even if it's too warm for skating this year, you can create an Ice Skating Scene to celebrate the outdoor fun. After that, why not invite friends to share Spicy Cake Donuts, Hot Caramel Apple Cider and all their recollections of chilly, cheery days on the ice?

Knit Tree Skirt instructions are on page 122.

Knit Skate Ornament

Knit Mitten

Knit Scarf

Knit Hat Ornament

Miniature sights of the season brighten a home with color and whimsy! Use self-striping yarn to knit skate, mitten and hat ornaments. Knit Scarf garlands also help warm the tree. The Ice Skating Scene is a beautiful way to enjoy memories of gliding on ice.

Knit Hat Ornament
Knit Mitten (Ornament)
Knit Scarf (Garland)
Knit Skate Ornament
Instructions begin on page 122.

Ice Skating Scene
Instructions are on page 127.

Lace 'em tight!

Winter fun calls for special ways to keep toasty! Spicy Cake Donuts and Hot Caramel Apple Cider will keep young folks warm on the inside, while a child-size Knit Scarf and Knit Mittens will chase the chill outside.

Hot Caramel Apple Cider

Fill a slow cooker before going out for a shopping trip...the spicy aroma will fill the house!

1/2 gal. apple cider
3/4 c. brown sugar, packed
1 1/2 t. cider vinegar
1 t. vanilla extract
4-inch cinnamon stick
6 whole cloves
1 orange, sliced
1/3 c. caramel ice cream topping

Combine all ingredients except topping in a slow cooker. Cover; cook on low setting for 5 to 6 hours. Strain; discard spices and orange. Serve in mugs, drizzling a teaspoonful of topping into each mug. Makes 7 1/2 cups.

Kimberly Hancock
Murrieta, CA

Spicy Cake Donuts

After ice skating or sledding, enjoy these donuts served with warm apple cider, cocoa or cinnamon tea.

3 1/4 c. all-purpose flour
2 t. baking powder
1 1/2 t. cinnamon, divided
1/2 t. salt
2 eggs
1 1/3 c. sugar, divided
1 t. vanilla extract
2/3 c. whipping cream
1/4 c. butter, melted

Combine flour, baking powder, one teaspoon cinnamon and salt. Beat together eggs, 2/3 cup sugar and vanilla until thick and lemon colored. Combine cream and butter. Alternately add dry ingredients and cream mixture to egg mixture. Beat each time until just blended. Chill dough for 2 hours.

Combine remaining 2/3 cup sugar and remaining 1/2 teaspoon cinnamon in a resealable plastic freezer bag; set aside. Roll out dough 3/8-inch thick on a floured surface. Cut with donut cutter. Fry in 375-degree oil, turning once; allow about one minute per side. Drain on paper towels. Shake warm donuts in bag with sugar and cinnamon. Makes about 17 donuts and holes.

Liz Roundtree
Petersburg, AK

Knit Mitten (Child Size)
Knit Scarf (Child Size)
Instructions begin on page 123.

Hot Caramel Apple Cider
Spicy Cake Donuts

Knit Mitten
Knit Scarf

I have the fondest memories of meeting friends to skate on Nancy Denning's pond in Connecticut (I'm the one in the light blue sweater, above). The first time I went, I didn't know how to skate. Nancy's dad held my hands while he skated backward and offered instruction. Soon I was skating on my own, pushing a metal lawn chair for balance. Whenever we skated, we had a great time. Nancy's mom would bring out warm donuts and tart cider. Her timing was always perfect; we had frozen toes and noses and were so hungry! Donuts never tasted better. I don't know how many winter days we spent on that frozen pond or how many donuts we ate, but those memories always make me smile.

Anne Pulliam Stocks
Little Rock, AR

43

Sharing the Best of Christmas

The best gifts of Christmas are the ones that show how much you care! Make thoughtful presents such as a Personalized Apron for a young cook, a soothing Neck Warmer to ease someone's aches or a thoughtful Hankie Blankie for a lover of vintage linens. Your friends & family will be delighted by the affection you put into each present!

Personalized Apron instructions begin on page 127.

Personalized Apron

Tag sale linens and potholders make oh-so-pretty Hanging Tea Towels, while fabric scraps sew up quickly into a microwaveable Neck Warmer. The JOY Banner is easy layers of fabric and felt.

Hanging Tea Towels

- vintage linens
- vintage crocheted potholders
- clear nylon thread
- buttons
- ribbons

Rescue vintage linens and turn them into hanging tea towels for your favorite cooks. Cut 16"x18" linen pieces; turn the raw edges 1/4" to the wrong side twice and hem. Baste along the top edge. Gathering to fit, pin each towel along the back bottom edges of a potholder. Zigzag using nylon thread. Sew a button to the front of each potholder (for our cherry print towel, we added a button "cherry" with crocheted leaves found in the scrapbooking section of the craft store). Sew a ribbon loop to the back for each hanger.

Hanging Tea Towels

Neck Warmer

JOY Banner

- water-soluble fabric marker
- white felt
- pinking shears
- red and green print fabrics
- cotton swab
- fabric glue
- ribbon
- jumbo rickrack

Share the JOY this season! Enlarge the patterns on page 152 to 250%; cut out the letters and one of each size circle. Drawing around the patterns with the marker, cut small and large felt circles. Use pinking shears to cut medium circles from red fabric. Cut green fabric circles slightly smaller than the small felt circles. Cut a letter from the center of each small felt circle. Dab away any marker lines with a damp cotton swab. Layer and glue the circles together; add bows at the top. Glue the circles to a rickrack garland.

Neck Warmer

- fabric scraps (we used 5 fabrics at least 9" long)
- two 10" lengths of 1"w grosgrain ribbon
- flannel for backing
- uncooked rice
- embroidery floss

A cozy gift for cold nights or tired muscles! Match right sides and use a ¹/₂" seam allowance unless otherwise noted. Wash and press all fabrics before beginning. Make the warmer as long as you like (the finished size of our neck wrap is 7"x17").

(continued on page 128)

JOY Banner

Vintage linens are pretty & practical when you sew them into a Bedside Catchall or a feminine Hankie Blankie.

Bedside Catchall

Give an embroidered heirloom that will be enjoyed...and well used! Press the open end of a pillowcase about 10" toward the closed end. Topstitch the side edges together. Sew up the middle of the pillowcase, creating pockets. Sew a button at the top of each line of stitching. Tuck the closed end between the mattress and box springs for a cozy catchall.

Hankie Blankie
- 1⅛ yards of muslin
- 7 vintage hankies (we used 2 more as embellishments)
- clear nylon thread
- one 12½"x12½" square each of 8 vintage-look fabrics (we pieced one square, trimming with rickrack over the seams)
- assorted fabric scraps for yo-yo's
- ribbon for leaves
- embroidery floss
- 1⅞ yards of backing fabric (wraps to front for binding)
- baby size cotton batting

Match right sides and use a ½" seam allowance unless otherwise noted. Our finished blankie is 37"x60".

(continued on page 128)

Bedside Catchall

48

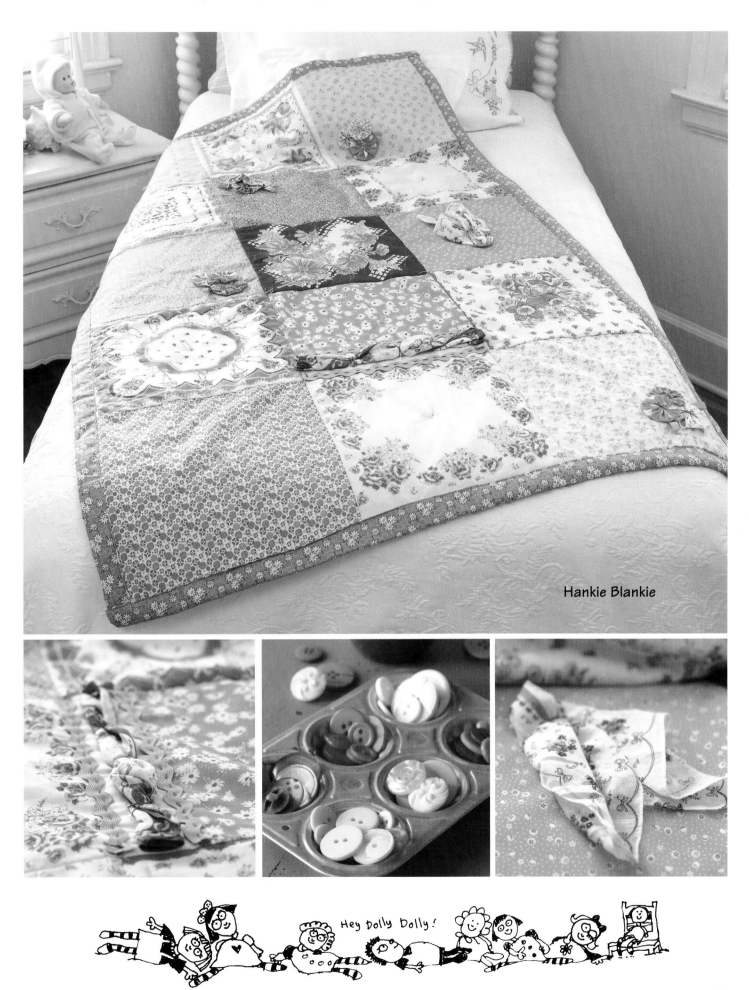

Hankie Blankie

Hey Dolly Dolly!

Keepsake Bracelet

Create a charm bracelet that highlights the life of someone special (we even added a state charm to showcase her birthplace). Start with a vintage bracelet chain and use jump rings and needle-nose jewelry pliers to add a mixture of charms from Mom's jewelry box, flea markets and new charms (see *Working with Jump Rings*, page 138). Fill tiny frames with dear photos. Earring dangles, beads on eye pins and a silk ribbon bow add plenty of color and personality!

Keepsake Bracelet

Posy Pendant

Posy Pendant

- water-soluble fabric marker
- tissue paper
- 5" linen square
- embroidery floss
- white paper for backing
- 1½"x1⅞" photo pendant with top and bottom loops
- ½" and ⅛"w ribbons
- beads
- flower charm
- 1" fancy head pin
- needle-nose jewelry pliers

Embroider your own or use a small vintage linen remnant to make a very special necklace.

1. Use the pattern on page 152 and follow the *Water-Soluble Fabric Marker Method* (page 138) to transfer the design to the linen square. Work *Stem Stitch* (page 139) stems and *Lazy Daisy* petals and leaves using 2 strands of floss.

2. Place the embroidered piece and a paper backing piece between the clear pendant inserts; trim to fit and insert in the pendant. Run the wide ribbon through the top loop of the pendant and tie narrow ribbons to the bottom loop.

3. To add the dangle, thread beads and the charm onto the head pin. Curl the end through the bottom pendant loop with pliers.

A meaningful piece of jewelry is always appreciated, especially when it's a Keepsake Bracelet or a Posy Pendant. The Wrist Corsage Pincushion makes sewing easier...and more fun!

Wrist Corsage Pincushion

- fabric scrap
- polyester fiberfill
- embroidery floss
- 3/8"w elastic
- felt scrap
- pinking shears
- 1 1/2" to 2" dia. button (to prevent pins from poking through the bottom)
- buttons for flower center (ours are 5/8" and 3/4" dia.)

Delight a budding seamstress with this floral-shaped pincushion. To be extra crafty, measure her wrist ahead of time without her knowing!

1. Cut two 3 1/4" diameter fabric circles. Matching right sides and leaving an opening for turning, use a 1/4" seam allowance to sew the pieces together. Clip the curves and turn right side out. Stuff firmly and sew the opening closed.

2. To form petals, knot the end of a 6-strand length of floss and sew through the center of the pincushion from bottom to top. Loop the floss over the edge of the cushion and back up through the center, pulling the floss tight. Repeat to make a total of 8 petals. Knot and trim the floss end.

3. Cut elastic to fit snugly around the wrist with a 1/2" overlap. Stretch the elastic and use pinking shears to cut a 3/4"w felt strip this length. Stretching the elastic as you go, sew the elastic along the center of the felt. Overlap and sew the ends together.

4. Sew the elastic loop between the bottom of the cushion and the large button. Sew the layered buttons to the top.

Wrist Corsage Pincushion

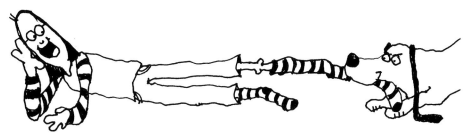

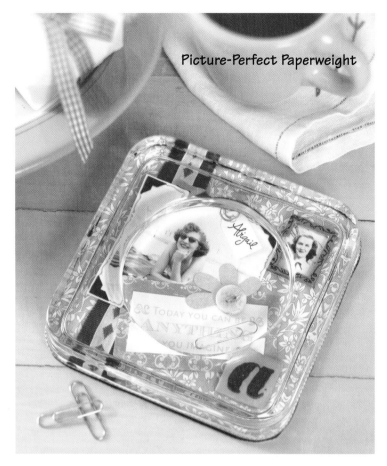

Picture-Perfect Paperweight

Picture-Pefect Paperweight

- flat glass candleholder (found at craft stores)
- tracing paper
- scrapbook paper
- poster board
- felt
- spray adhesive
- clear-drying glue
- memorabilia (we used ribbons, photos, a quote, tag, paperclip, chipboard letter, flower charm and button)
- 1/8"w ribbon

1. Draw around the base of the candleholder on tracing paper. Use the pattern to cut a piece each from scrapbook paper, poster board and felt.
2. Using spray adhesive in a well-ventilated area, sandwich the poster board between the scrapbook paper and felt pieces.
3. Arrange and glue memorabilia to the scrapbook paper. Glue the outer edge of the paper to the candleholder bottom. Glue 1/8" ribbon along the bottom side edge to finish.

Felt Fob

- tracing paper
- water-soluble fabric marker
- fabric scrap
- felt scraps (including cream & blue for backgrounds)
- pinking shears
- embroidery floss
- fabric glue
- key ring
- button

1. Trace the patterns on page 152. Refer to the photo and use the patterns to cut the small hill from fabric and the remaining shapes from felt, using pinking shears as desired.
2. Pin the flowers on the cream background.
3. Refer to the pattern and key and use 6 strands of floss to work *Stem Stitch* (page 139) stems, *Lazy Daisy* leaves and *Straight Stitch*, *Backstitch* and *French Knot* flower details. Add *Running Stitches* around the top and side edges of the cream background piece.
4. Glue the hill pieces in place. Fold a 1/2"x2 1/2" felt tab in half around the key ring. Glue the ends to the back of the cream piece and glue to the blue background piece. Add the button, sewing through all layers.

Felt Fob

Flap Cap

For anyone who enjoys springtime flowers, the Felt Fob is a welcome gift. A Picture-Perfect Paperweight will please a loved one with the sight of a collage created in his or her honor. You can also transform a frame into a Snowbound Tray, or crochet a Flap Cap to keep a special boy warm & toasty.

Flap Cap
Read Crochet on pages 142-143 before beginning.

■■□□ **EASY**

Finished Size: 15" (38 cm) head circumference

Materials
Medium Weight Yarn [MEDIUM **4**]
    [3 ounces, 145 yards
    (85 grams, 133 meters) per
    skein]: 1 skein
Crochet hook, size I (5.5 mm) **or** size
    needed for gauge

(continued on page 129)

Snowbound Tray
• 11"x14" whitewashed wood frame
  with glass and a sturdy backing
• screwdriver
• drawer pulls
• craft glue
• scrapbook papers
• acid-free marker
• ribbons
• green and black cardstock
• white crayon

(continued on page 129)

Snowbound Tray

Give it with a festive flair!

You have the best gifts for everyone near and dear, so now it's time for the perfect presentations! The Country Friends gathered these extra-cheery ideas for gift boxes, tags, greeting cards and a gift card holder. Special ideas include a scrapbooker's supply caddy and new boots in bright colors! And here's a fun way to spend time with friends this Christmas...invite them to a gift tag exchange!

Monogrammed Package and Cherry Box & Tag instructions begin on page 130.

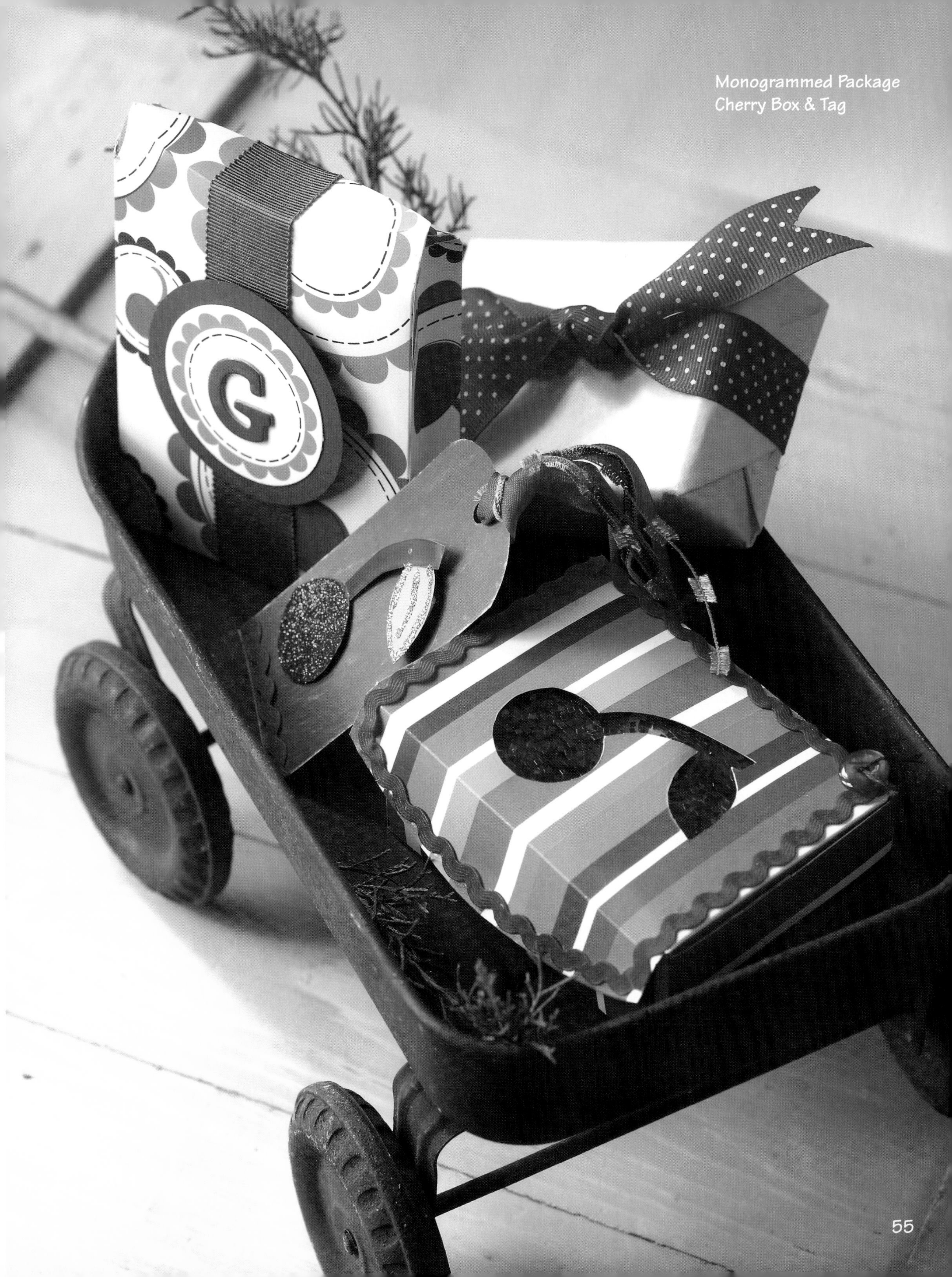

Monogrammed Package
Cherry Box & Tag

Oval Gift Box

- oval papier-mâché box (ours is 5¹/₂"x7")
- red, green and ivory acrylic paints
- paintbrushes
- round foam brush
- sandpaper
- hot glue gun or double-sided tape
- vintage crocheted potholder
- vintage letter squares

Paint the box and lid; then, add polka dots with the round brush. Sand the edges for an aged appearance. Hot glue or tape the vintage potholder to the lid and add a name or initials on top.

Square Gift Box

Instructions are on page 131.

Photo Cards

Giving photo cards will rekindle warm memories. Use double-sided tape to mat a copy of a favorite photo postcard on scrapbook paper. Cut and fold a card from cardstock-backed paper. Adhere rickrack with fabric glue; then, tape the photo in place. Hot glue self-covered buttons and a vintage-look ribbon bow to the card.

For a perfect backdrop to a 3" square photo, fold a 4¹/₂"x9" piece of cardstock-backed scrapbook paper in half; unfold. Pierce holes with a sewing needle every ¹/₂" along the fold and ¹/₂" in from the front edges. Using 6 stands of embroidery floss, work Blanket Stitches (page 139) around the edges. Mount the photo with photo corners. Add the year of the photo and a jeweled brad to a tag; adhere to the card with an adhesive foam dot.

Photo Cards

Fabric Tree Card

- cardstock
- fabric glue
- mini rickrack
- fabric scrap
- embroidery floss
- tiny buttons with flat-ended shanks
- square button

Make a card to be treasured by your favorite stitcher. Match short ends and fold a 6¹⁄₂"x10" cardstock piece in half. Glue rickrack along the top and bottom of the card front. Glue simple fabric leaves to the card in a tree shape. Tie a floss length through each button. Glue the shank buttons to the tree and the square button "trunk" at the bottom.

Redbird Collage Card

- white cardstock
- scrapbook papers
- white and colored tissue papers
- disposable foam brush
- decoupage glue
- sharp needle
- embroidery floss
- ribbon

Express yourself with a collage of your favorite papers. Matching short ends, fold a 7"x10" cardstock piece in half. Enlarge the pattern on page 152 to 143%. Using the pattern, cut a scrapbook paper bird. Cut different size leaves and circles from scrapbook and tissue papers. Arrange the shapes on the card front; adhere with a thin layer of glue. Allowing to dry between coats, brush 2 more coats of glue on the card front. Pierce evenly-spaced holes and use 2 strands of floss to work *Running Stitches* (page 139) along the top of the card. Add a bow at the top.

For gift boxes and greeting cards that are a present in themselves, create these oh-so-thoughtful ideas!

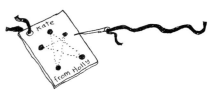

Fabric Tree Card
Redbird Collage Card
Pull-Tab Gift Card Holder

Pull-Tab Gift Card Holder

- cardstock scraps
- fabric glue
- fabric scraps
- sharp needle
- embroidery floss
- ³⁄₈"w twill tape
- purchased gift card
- jewelry tag

This clever idea works for any gift card; simply adjust the size of the holder to fit (our card is 2¹⁄₈"x3³⁄₈").

Matching short ends, fold a 3"x8" cardstock piece in half. Glue layered fabric circles and a cardstock "ornament cap" to the front of the holder; unfold. Pierce holes and use 3 strands of floss to work a *Running Stitch* (page 139) "hanger." Refold the holder and machine stitch ¹⁄₈" from the side edges. Tie twill tape around the gift card and add a tiny tag.

Get your crafty friends together for the fun of a gift tag exchange! Before the party, the hostess and each guest make enough blank gift tags to share with everyone else. As the party begins, the tags are sorted into pretty mugs. Each guest takes home one mug filled with a variety of handmade tags, as well as great memories of time shared with friends! Instructions to make three Gift Tags and the paper Garland begin on page 131.

Nutty Popcorn Snack Mix

If you're using microwave popcorn, simply pop two, 3½-oz. packages.

16 c. popped popcorn
5 c. mini pretzel twists
1 c. dry-roasted peanuts
2 c. brown sugar, packed
½ c. margarine
½ c. dark corn syrup
¼ t. salt
1 t. vanilla extract
½ t. baking soda
1½ c. mini candy-coated
    chocolate pieces

Combine popcorn, pretzels and peanuts in a large roasting pan; set aside.

Combine brown sugar, margarine, corn syrup and salt in a heavy medium saucepan. Cook over medium heat for 12 to 14 minutes, stirring occasionally, until mixture comes to a full boil. Continue cooking and stirring until mixture reaches the soft-ball stage, or 234 to 240 degrees on a candy thermometer. Remove from heat; stir in vanilla and baking soda. Pour over popcorn mixture in roasting pan; stir until mixture is well coated.

Bake at 250 degrees for 45 minutes, stirring every 15 minutes. Immediately spoon onto wax paper; let cool 10 minutes and sprinkle with chocolate pieces. Cool completely; break into pieces. Store in an airtight container. Makes about 24 cups.

Raspberry Cider

Snuggle in with a cup of this fruity cider.

1 qt. apple cider
2 c. water
1 c. raspberry jelly
1 t. sweetened lemonade drink mix
Garnish: lemon slices

Bring cider and water to a boil in a 3-quart saucepan; add jelly and drink mix. Stir until jelly dissolves; remove from heat. Pour into serving mugs while still warm; garnish with lemon slices. Makes 6 cups.

Sue Osburn
Hot Springs, AR

Gift Tags and Garland

Instructions begin on page 131.

Nutty Popcorn Snack Mix
Raspberry Cider

Gift Tags

Garland

Fun-Filled Containers

These delightful alternatives to gift wrap are as fun to give as they are to receive!

Scrapbook Caddy

- ½ yard of 72"w red felt
- pinking shears
- water-soluble fabric marker
- tissue paper (optional)
- embroidery floss
- assorted 2-hole buttons
- scrapbook supplies
- 1⁵/₈ yards of ³/₈"w ribbon

The perfect package for your favorite scrapbooker! Match wrong sides and use a ¼" seam allowance unless otherwise noted.

1. Cut the following pieces from felt: two 10½"x9" dividers, two 11"x7" bottoms, four 7"x5" sides and four 11"x5" front/back pieces.
2. Enlarge the patterns on page 153 to 222%. Using the divider pattern, cut away the top curve and hole for the handle on both divider pieces. Sew the pieces together along all edges. Pink the top edge.

(continued on page 132)

Glass Canisters

Scrapbook Caddy

Personalized Photo Box

60

For wonderfully whimsical presentations, put gifts in the Scrapbook Caddy and other Fun-Filled Containers. The recipients will know how very special they are to you!

Glass Canisters

Turn a new glass jar into a treasured memory keeper. Lightly sand, then paint the lid of each square jar (we used red and green acrylic paints). Sand the edges for a vintage look. Fill the jars with cookie cutters and potholders or childhood toys. Tie pre-printed twill tape (ours says "Holiday Hugs") around the cookie cutter jar and add a die-cut label to the front. For the toy jar, hot glue an alphabet block to the top and use adhesive foam dots to add a name to the front with vintage or chipboard letter squares.

Personalized Photo Box

- sandpaper
- solid color photo box
- wax paper
- thick craft glue
- wood bead garland
- acrylic paint
- paintbrush
- papier-mâché letter (first letter of name)
- patterned cardstock
- pinking shears
- spray adhesive
- decorative chipboard letters (the rest of the name)
- buttons

A special package for any gift, the photo box is a must-have for a camera buff!

1. Sand the edges of the box and lid for an aged appearance. Place the lid on wax paper. Glue the garland around the lid and allow to dry.

2. Paint the top edge and sides of the papier-mâché letter. Trace the letter onto the back of cardstock and cut out with pinking shears. Using spray adhesive in a well-ventilated area, attach the cardstock letter. Glue the remaining letters and buttons in place. Glue the letter to the box lid.

Shiny New Boots

Shiny New Boots

Like a stocking, only twice the joy! Fill up a new pair of child's wellies with gifts and trinkets. Tuck in small packages and vintage toys along with candy canes and greenery sprigs. Add a mini ornament and Christmas charm to a layered cardstock tag. What fun!

CRAFTY KID STUFF

The kids in your life will love creating these fun decorations and gifts! With your help, they'll use a few easy stitches to make a cheery Fleece Scarf & Hat Set or little Felt Gift Bags. Wooden thread spools quickly become an adorable family of spool people, while the whimsical Chubby Chirpers begin with purchased papier-mâché shapes. And not only are the Hanging Birdfeeder and Bag o' Birdseed great gifts to make, they're also projects that teach youngsters to care for our feathered friends!

Fleece Scarf & Hat Set instructions begin on page 132.

Fleece Scarf & Hat Set

Spool Family

Spool Family

- scrapbook papers
- vintage wooden thread spools (ours range from 1¹/₈" to 1³/₄" tall)
- unfinished wood wheel (same diameter as largest spool)
- craft glue
- low-temp glue gun
- wood doll heads (ours are 1", 1¹/₄" and two 1¹/₂" dia.)
- acrylic paints
- paintbrushes
- embroidery floss
- fleece scraps
- 10mm pom-poms
- felt scraps
- chenille stems

(continued on page 133)

Felt Gift Bags, Hanging Birdfeeder and Bag o' Birdseed

Instructions begin on page 133.

Felt Gift Bags

Hanging Birdfeeder and Bag o' Birdseed

The Felt Gift Bags are made with simple stitches, while the Spool Family, Hanging Birdfeeder and Chubby Chirpers are easy to assemble and decorate with paint, paper and other fun items!

Chubby Chirpers

- acrylic paints
- paintbrushes
- papier-mâché pears (ours are 3¹/₂" to 4" tall)
- clothespins
- low-temp glue gun
- chenille stems (we used bump and regular stems)
- tracing paper
- felt and print fabric scraps
- scallop-edged fabric scissors
- fabric glue
- wiggle eyes
- buttons

A fun and easy craft…let a grown-up help attach the crest and clothespin with the glue gun. Use fabric glue everywhere else.

1. For each bird, refer to *Drybrushing* (page 138) to paint a pear and clothespin using contrasting colors. Remove the pear stem; then, shape and glue a chenille stem crest in its place with the glue gun.
2. Using the patterns on page 154, cut a felt beak and large tail. Cut 2 fabric wings and a small tail. Scallop the curved edges of the wing and tail shapes.
3. Layer and glue the tail shapes together at the base. Pinch pleat the center of the base and glue the tail to the bird. Glue the wiggle eyes, beak, pointed wing ends and buttons to the bird.
4. Use the glue gun to attach the clothespin to the bird.

Chubby Chirpers

Gifts of Goodness from the Kitchen

Delicious, comforting foods made with love…what better gifts could anyone give or receive? These yummy wishes for a Merry Christmas are especially nice when presented in special boxes, jars and other containers. Make a batch of Mom's Applesauce Muffins to give in decorated Muffin Tins. Or stir up Savory Rice Mix and attach the recipe to a gift jar. You can help a busy cook serve a holiday treat with a gift of Banana Supreme Pie in a Pie Carrier. Round out your gift list with these tasty treats!

Mom's Applesauce Muffins
Muffin Tin

Mom's Applesauce Muffins

Fill your kitchen with the delectable aroma of apples and cinnamon.

1/2 c. butter, softened
1 c. sugar
1 c. applesauce
1 egg, beaten
2 c. all-purpose flour
1 t. baking soda
1 t. cinnamon
1/2 t. ground cloves
1/4 t. salt
1 c. raisins

Combine butter, sugar, applesauce and egg. In a separate bowl, combine flour, baking soda, cinnamon, cloves and salt; stir into butter mixture just until moistened. Stir in raisins. Fill paper-lined muffin cups 3/4 full; sprinkle with crumb topping. Bake at 350 degrees for 25 to 30 minutes. Makes 12 to 16.

Crumb Topping:
1/2 c. butter, softened
3/4 c. all-purpose flour
3/4 c. quick-cooking oats, uncooked
1/2 c. brown sugar, packed
2 t. cinnamon

Blend all ingredients until crumbly.

Emily Johnson
Pocatello, ID

Muffin Tin instructions are on page 135.

Graham Cracker Fudge
Fudge Box

Treat a favorite chocolate lover with a colorful Fudge Box of Graham Cracker Fudge. For warm beverage fans, give Snickerdoodle Coffee Mix in a fun Coffee Canister.

Graham Cracker Fudge

My mother wrote down her favorite fudge recipe for me on the first Christmas I was married (over 40 years ago). She saved the original clipping cut from a November 1942 magazine. Now I have both copies...they are yellowed with time, but the fudge is as delicious and chewy as ever.

2 sqs. unsweetened baking
    chocolate
14-oz. can sweetened condensed
    milk
½ t. vanilla extract
1¾ c. graham crackers, finely
    crushed
1½ c. chopped pecans, walnuts
    or almonds, divided

Melt chocolate in a double boiler over hot water. Add condensed milk and cook, stirring constantly, about 5 minutes or until mixture thickens. Add vanilla, graham cracker crumbs and one cup nuts; mix well. Sprinkle ¼ cup of remaining nuts in the bottom of a buttered 8"x8" baking pan. Use a knife that has been dipped in hot water to spread chocolate mixture in pan. Press remaining ¼ cup nuts into top. Cover and chill overnight. Cut into squares. Makes 16.

Nancy Otto
Indiana, PA

Fudge Box instructions are on page 135.

Snickerdoodle Coffee Mix

A chocolatey drink all your co-workers will appreciate.

1 c. sugar
1 c. powdered milk
1/2 c. vanilla-flavored powdered
    non-dairy creamer
1/2 c. baking cocoa
3 T. instant coffee granules
1/2 t. allspice
1/4 t. cinnamon

Combine all ingredients; store in an airtight container. Give with instructions. Makes about 3 cups mix.

Instructions: Add 3 tablespoons mix to 3/4 cup boiling water; stir well. Makes one serving.

Coffee Canister

- plastic zipping bag filled with Snickerdoodle Coffee Mix
- canister (ours is 5"hx4" dia.)
- pinking shears
- holiday scrapbook papers
- craft knife and cutting mat
- assorted fabric and felt scraps
- large yarn needle
- decorative brad
- 3/8"w ribbon
- jute twine
- chipboard tag with recipient's initial
- rub-on letters
- scrapbook paper label
- double-sided tape

1. Place the coffee mix in the canister.
2. Use pinking shears to cut a 2 1/2" and a 3 1/2" diameter scrapbook paper circle. Cut a 1/2"-long slit about 1" in from opposite sides of the larger circle for the ribbon to run through. Cut three 3" diameter circles from fabric and 2 from felt.
3. Center the 3" circles between the paper circles. Use the needle to pierce a hole through all layers and join the circles with the brad. Thread the ribbon through the slits in the large paper circle and knot at the bottom of the canister.
4. Use twine to tie the initial tag around the brad beneath the fabric.
5. Use rub-ons to add individual serving instructions to the label. Tape the label to the canister.

**Snickerdoodle Coffee Mix
Coffee Canister**

Honey Popcorn & Cashews in a Party Mix Tin will thrill anyone who likes their snacks sweet & salty. Be sure to keep one jar of Carrot Cake Jam for yourself!

Honey Popcorn & Cashews

This recipe came from a dear neighbor when we first moved to our new home in 1977. My 3 sons just loved it. It is very addictive and always a hit.

3 qts. popped popcorn
1¹/₂ c. cashews
1 c. sugar
¹/₂ c. honey
¹/₂ c. light corn syrup
1 c. creamy peanut butter
1 t. vanilla extract

Toss together popped popcorn and cashews in a large roaster pan; keep warm in a 250-degree oven.

In a heavy 1¹/₂-quart saucepan, combine sugar, honey and corn syrup. Bring mixture to a rapid boil over medium heat, stirring constantly; boil for 2 minutes. Remove from heat; stir in peanut butter and vanilla. Immediately pour over popcorn mixture, stirring to coat thoroughly. Spread on greased aluminum foil to cool. Break into bite-size pieces. Makes 5 quarts.

Diane Garber
Brookville, OH

Party Mix Tin instructions begin on page 135.

Honey Popcorn & Cashews
Party Mix Tin

Carrot Cake Jam

*This is a wonderful jam that tastes
just like Grandma's carrot cake!*

1¹/₂ c. carrots, peeled and
    shredded
1¹/₂ c. pears, cored, peeled and
    chopped
14-oz. can crushed pineapple
3 T. lemon juice
1¹/₂ t. cinnamon
1 t. nutmeg
1 t. ground cloves
3-oz. pouch liquid pectin
6¹/₂ c. sugar
6 ¹/₂-pint canning jars and lids,
    sterilized

Mix all ingredients except
pectin and sugar in a large
saucepan. Bring to a boil over
medium heat. Reduce heat
to medium-low; simmer for
20 minutes, stirring occasionally.
Add pectin and return to a boil.
Stir in sugar; bring to a full rolling
boil, stirring constantly. Remove
from heat. Pour into hot sterilized
jars, leaving ¹/₂-inch headspace.
Secure with lids. Cool and store in
refrigerator up to 3 weeks. Makes
6 jars.

*Teri Johnson
North Ogden, UT*

Jam Jar

Color photocopy the label on
page 154 onto white cardstock;
cut out. Use double-sided tape
to adhere the label to a vintage-
look jar of Carrot Cake Jam. Tie a
coordinating ribbon around the lid.
What a yummy gift!

Cherry-Chocolate Chip Loaves mix the sweetness of bananas with the zip of dried cherries. It's easy to stamp the Loaf Tin with snowflakes. For a side dish everyone will enjoy, combine rice and seasonings to make Savory Rice Mix. You'll have fun decorating the Rice Mix Jar with a recipe pocket!

Loaf Tin

- acrylic paints for metal
- white tin with hinged lid (ours is 7"wx4"dx5"h)
- foam stamps and round foam brushes
- craft glue
- cardstock
- magnetic photo frame (ours is 3¼"x2¼")
- rub-on letters
- hole punch
- scallop-edged scissors
- 2 plastic-wrapped Cherry-Chocolate Chip Loaves
- ribbons

Using paints, stamp the sides and lid of the tin with foam stamps and brushes. Make a layered cardstock label to fit in the magnetic photo frame using rub-ons and punched cardstock dots (we scalloped the edges of the top cardstock piece). Place the loaves in the tin and tie ribbons around the handle.

Cherry-Chocolate Chip Loaves
Loaf Tin

Cherry-Chocolate Chip Loaves

Try substituting sweetened dried cranberries for the cherries...a bit tangy, but just as yummy.

½ c. butter, softened
1 c. sugar
1 c. ripe banana, mashed
2 eggs, beaten
2 c. all-purpose flour
1 t. baking soda
¼ c. chopped walnuts
¼ c. mini semi-sweet chocolate chips
¼ c. dried cherries, chopped

Blend together butter and sugar in a large bowl. Add banana and eggs; mix well. In a separate bowl, combine flour and baking soda; gradually add to butter mixture. Fold in walnuts, chocolate chips and cherries. Transfer to 4 greased 5½"x3" loaf pans. Bake at 350 degrees for 32 to 37 minutes or until a toothpick inserted near center comes out clean. Cool for 10 minutes before removing from pans to wire racks. Makes 4 mini loaves.

Vickie

Savory Rice Mix

Altogether, this great gift makes about 16 tasty side-dish servings!

4 c. long-cooking rice, uncooked
1/4 c. dried, minced onion
1 env. from a 2-oz. pkg. onion soup mix
1 T. dried parsley
1/4 t. garlic salt
1/4 t. salt

Combine all ingredients; store in an airtight container for up to 4 months. Give with instructions. Makes about 4 cups mix.

Instructions: Mix one cup mix with 2 cups beef broth in a 2-quart saucepan; add one tablespoon butter. Bring to a rolling boil; reduce heat. Simmer, covered, until liquid is absorbed, about 20 to 25 minutes. Makes 4 servings.

Rice Mix Jar instructions are on page 136.

Savory Rice Mix
Rice Mix Jar

Chocolate-Dipped Crispy Bars look like a gourmet gift in the clear Treat Container. Snowflake-embellished Paper Trays offer generous servings of chocolatey Rocky Road Bars.

Chocolate-Dipped Crispy Bars

Crunchy and sweet with a taste of peanut butter and chocolate!

6 c. crispy rice cereal
1 c. sugar
1 c. corn syrup
1 c. creamy peanut butter
12-oz. pkg. dark cocoa-flavored candy wafers, melted
1 c. semi-sweet chocolate chips, melted
1½ c. white chocolate-flavored candy wafers, melted

Place cereal in a large bowl; set aside.

In a heavy medium saucepan, combine sugar and corn syrup over medium-high heat; stir frequently until mixture boils. Allow to boil 30 seconds without stirring. Remove from heat and stir in peanut butter. Pour peanut butter mixture over cereal; stir until well blended. Press mixture into a 13"x9" baking pan; cool. Cut into 4"x1" bars. Combine next 2 ingredients. Dip half of each bar into dark chocolate mixture; place on wax paper until chocolate hardens. Drizzle white chocolate over dark chocolate and return to wax paper to harden. Makes 24.

Chocolate-Dipped Crispy Bars Treat Container

Treat Container
- double-sided holiday scrapbook paper
- clear acrylic container with handle and lid (ours is 6"hx4" dia.)
- wax paper
- Chocolate-Dipped Crispy Bars
- hole punch
- craft glue
- glitter
- jute twine, ribbon and rickrack trims
- rub-on letters
- double-sided tape

1. Insert a scrapbook paper piece in the container that fits around the inside and is half the container's height. Line with wax paper and place the bars in the container.
2. Cut a motif from scrapbook paper, punch a hole and add glitter; tie to the handle with trims.
3. Cut a scrapbook paper circle to fit the container top; add rub-ons and tape the circle to the lid.

Rocky Road Bars

Brownies with chocolate chips, marshmallows and peanuts...need I say more?

22¹/₂-oz. pkg. brownie mix with chocolate syrup pouch
¹/₃ c. oil
¹/₄ c. water
2 eggs, beaten
12-oz. pkg. semi-sweet chocolate chips, divided
1¹/₂ to 2 c. mini marshmallows
¹/₂ c. dry-roasted peanuts, chopped

Grease bottom only of a 13"x9" baking pan; set aside.

Combine brownie mix, syrup pouch, oil, water and eggs; stir until well blended. Mix in one cup chocolate chips; spread in baking pan. Bake at 350 degrees for 30 to 35 minutes or until a toothpick inserted 2 inches from side of pan comes out clean. Immediately sprinkle with marshmallows, remaining one cup chocolate chips and peanuts. Cover pan with a baking sheet for 2 to 3 minutes; remove and cool completely. Cut into 4"x2" bars; store tightly covered. Makes one dozen.

Dale-Harriet Rogovich
Madison, WI

Paper Trays instructions begin on page 136.

Rocky Road Bars
Paper Trays

Tangy Lemon Delights are a pecan-lover's ideal cookies. The Delight-full Box adds whimsy to the season with its fluffy yarn pom-pom. For a special presentation, give someone dear a Banana Supreme Pie in a decoupaged Pie Carrier.

Lemon Delights

These cookies are wonderful made with fresh Georgia pecans!

1 c. butter, softened
1 c. sugar
3-oz. pkg. cream cheese, softened
1 egg, separated
1 T. lemon juice
1 t. vanilla extract
1 t. lemon extract
¼ t. salt
2¼ c. all-purpose flour
2½ c. pecans, finely chopped

Combine butter, sugar, cream cheese, egg yolk, lemon juice, extracts and salt. Mix well with an electric mixer on medium speed; beat in flour. Wrap in plastic wrap; chill for at least one hour.

Form dough into one-inch balls. In a small bowl, beat egg white lightly. Dip balls into egg white; roll in pecans. Place 2 inches apart on ungreased baking sheets. Press thumb deeply into center of each cookie. Spoon lemon cheese filling into indents. Bake at 375 degrees for 8 to 10 minutes or until filling is set. Cool slightly; remove to a wire rack. Keep refrigerated in an airtight container. Makes 6 dozen.

Lemon Cheese Filling:
3-oz. pkg. cream cheese, softened
¼ c. sugar
1 egg yolk
1 T. lemon juice
1 t. lemon extract
1 drop yellow food coloring

Beat together all ingredients until smooth.

Tracey Varela
Thomasville, GA

Delight-full Box instructions are on page 137.

Banana Supreme Pie

Shh...don't tell anyone how easy this is to make!

1 c. sour cream
1/2 c. milk
3.4-oz. pkg. instant vanilla pudding mix
8-oz. container frozen whipped
    topping, thawed
3/4 c. peanuts, chopped and divided
10-inch graham cracker crust
1 to 2 ripe bananas, sliced

Stir together sour cream, milk and pudding mix. Fold in whipped topping; set aside.

Sprinkle 1/2 cup peanuts on bottom of pie crust; arrange banana slices on peanuts. Spoon pudding mixture over bananas; sprinkle with remaining 1/4 cup peanuts. Cover and chill until ready to serve. Makes 8 servings.

Regina Kostyu
Gooseberry Patch

Pie Carrier

- mat board
- craft knife and cutting mat
- 13" dia. papier-mâché plate (ours has a 9½" bottom)
- acrylic paints
- paintbrush
- 2⅜"h chipboard letters (PIE)
- decoupage glue
- disposable foam brush
- assorted Christmas wrapping papers
- glittered star stickers
- mica flakes
- 3½ yards of 1½"w ribbon
- assorted ribbons
- vintage miniature ornaments
- Banana Supreme Pie

(continued on page 137)

To be BUSY is man's only *happiness.*
—MARK TWAIN—

Banana Supreme Pie
Pie Carrier

casual Holiday gathering

Getting together with family & friends to share the holiday spirit is so much fun! For these casual meals, it's nice to offer a mix of traditional recipes and new dishes that are sure to become comfort-food favorites. Serve a delicious Cranberry-Glazed Ham with Parmesan Pull-Aparts, Prize-Winning Pineapple Cheddar Bake and Garlicky Green Beans. Still a little time before dinner's ready? Crabby Artichoke Spread is yummy on crackers or toasted bread rounds, and it will please your hungry crowd until time to set the table. Don't forget the melt-in-your-mouth Chocolate Chess Pie for dessert!

Cranberry-Glazed Ham

Cranberry-Glazed Ham

Serve slices topped with a generous spoonful of the brown sugar-cranberry glaze...wonderful!

5 to 6-lb. ham
16-oz. can jellied cranberry sauce
1 c. brown sugar, packed
¼ c. orange juice
½ t. ground cloves
¼ t. cinnamon
¼ t. allspice

Bake ham at 350 degrees for 18 to 20 minutes per pound or until meat thermometer registers 160 degrees. While ham is baking, combine remaining ingredients in a saucepan; heat slowly, whisking until smooth. Spoon half the glaze mixture over the ham 30 minutes before removing it from the oven; continue baking for 30 minutes. Serve with remaining glaze. Serves 8 to 10.

Beverly Smith
Malin, OR

Garlicky Green Beans, Prize-Winning Pineapple Cheddar Bake and Parmesan Pull-Aparts are the perfect accompaniments for Cranberry-Glazed Ham (page 79). Start the meal with tangy Spinach & Clementine Salad.

Garlicky Green Beans

Crispy-tender green beans cooked with the flavor of garlic...a wonderful side dish.

3 lbs. green beans
1/2 c. olive oil
9 cloves garlic, crushed
1/2 c. fresh parsley, chopped
1 c. dry bread crumbs
3/4 c. grated Romano cheese

Steam green beans until crisp-tender; drain and set aside.

Heat oil in a large skillet; add garlic and parsley. Cook until garlic is lightly golden; add beans and cook, stirring, for 2 minutes. Remove from heat; discard garlic. Combine bread crumbs and cheese; sprinkle over beans. Serves 8 to 10.

Melanie Lowe
Dover, DE

Prize-Winning Pineapple Cheddar Bake

This recipe has been in my family for a very long time and I even won 2nd place when I entered it in a Dairy Council contest.

2 20-oz. cans pineapple tidbits
8-oz. pkg. shredded Cheddar cheese
1 c. sugar
3/4 c. all-purpose flour
1 sleeve round buttery crackers, crushed
1/4 c. margarine, melted

Mix together pineapple, cheese, sugar and flour; spread into a greased 2-quart casserole. Combine cracker crumbs and margarine; sprinkle over pineapple mixture. Bake, covered, at 350 degrees for 30 minutes. Serve hot or cold. Makes 8 servings.

Marta May
Anderson, IN

Parmesan Pull-Aparts

Three kinds of savory seeds really dress up ordinary biscuits.

3 T. margarine
1 T. onion, minced
2 t. dill seed
1 t. poppy seed
1/4 t. celery seed
12-oz. tube refrigerated biscuits, quartered
1/4 c. grated Parmesan cheese

Melt margarine in a 9" round cake pan. Sprinkle onion, dill, poppy and celery seed over margarine. Sprinkle quartered biscuits with cheese and arrange in pan. Bake at 400 degrees for 15 to 18 minutes. To serve, invert pan over a serving platter and turn out biscuits. Makes 10 servings.

Diane Cohen
Kennesaw, GA

Old-Fashioned Corn Pudding

It wouldn't be Christmas without this dish on our table...I usually double the recipe!

2 eggs, beaten
1/4 to 1/2 c. sugar
2 slices bread, crusts trimmed
14³/₄-oz. can creamed corn
1/2 c. evaporated milk
1 t. vanilla extract

Mix together eggs and sugar; cube bread and add to mixture. Stir in corn, milk and vanilla. Pour mixture into a buttered 1¹/₂-quart casserole dish. Bake at 350 degrees for one hour. Serves 4 to 6.

Jodi King
Friendship, MD

MAKE A TOAST WITH HOT CHOCOLATE IN WINE GLASSES!

Spinach & Clementine Salad

This fresh, crunchy salad is a perfect way to use a Christmas gift box of clementines.

2 lbs. clementines, peeled and sectioned
2 lbs. baby spinach
4 stalks celery, thinly sliced
1 c. red onion, thinly sliced
1/2 c. pine nuts or walnuts, toasted
1/4 c. dried cherries
1/4 c. olive oil
2 T. red wine vinegar
1 clove garlic, minced
1 t. Dijon mustard
1/8 t. sugar
salt and pepper to taste

Place clementines in a large salad bowl with spinach, celery, onion, nuts and cherries. Toss to mix well. Whisk together remaining ingredients in a small bowl; drizzle over salad. Serve immediately. Makes 8 servings.

Sharon Jones
Oklahoma City, OK

Welcome
SET UP A SWEET CANDY BAR!

Spinach & Clementine Salad

Please your crowd with the unexpected (and yummy!) flavors of Crabby Artichoke Spread, Roasted Brussels Sprouts, and Teri's Butternut Squash Soup.

Crabby Artichoke Spread

Roasted Brussels Sprouts
Orange zest and juice give these Brussels sprouts a pleasing hint of citrus.

1 T. orange juice
2 t. olive oil
1 t. grated orange zest
1 lb. Brussels sprouts, halved
non-stick vegetable spray
1/2 t. salt
1/4 t. pepper
Garnish: orange zest strips

Combine orange juice, olive oil and orange zest in a small bowl. Place Brussels sprouts on a jelly-roll pan coated with vegetable spray; drizzle orange juice mixture over sprouts and toss gently to coat. Sprinkle with salt and pepper. Bake at 450 degrees for 15 to 20 minutes or until edges of sprouts look lightly browned and crisp. Garnish, if desired. Makes 4 servings.

Crabby Artichoke Spread
Your guests will just love this creamy, spicy dip!

1 jalapeño pepper, seeded and chopped
1 t. oil
14-oz. can artichokes, drained and chopped
2 6-oz. cans crabmeat, drained
1 c. mayonnaise
1/2 red pepper, chopped
1/4 c. grated Parmesan cheese
2 green onions, chopped
2 t. lemon juice
2 t. Worcestershire sauce
1/2 t. celery seed
toasted bread rounds or crackers

Sauté jalapeño in oil until tender. Combine jalapeño and remaining ingredients except bread rounds in a slow cooker. Cover and cook on low setting for 4 hours. Serve with bread rounds or crackers. Makes 3 to 4 cups.

Kathy Grashoff
Fort Wayne, IN

Roasted Brussels Sprouts

Teri's Butternut Squash Soup

Cajun Spiced Pecans

Fill small ribbon-tied bags with these delightful nuts to send home with dinner guests as party favors.

16-oz. pkg. pecan halves
1/4 c. butter, melted
1 T. chili powder
1 t. dried basil
1 t. dried oregano
1 t. dried thyme
1 t. salt
1/2 t. onion powder
1/4 t. garlic powder
1/4 t. cayenne pepper

Combine all ingredients in a slow cooker. Cover and cook on high setting for 15 minutes. Turn to low setting and cook, uncovered, for 2 hours, stirring occasionally. Transfer nuts to a baking sheet; cool completely. Store in an airtight container. Serves 12 to 16.

Kerry Mayer
Dunham Springs, LA

Teri's Butternut Squash Soup

We tried a delicious squash soup at a local restaurant. This recipe is my own version and it's so good! We find it's also wonderful served chilled with sliced green onions on top.

1 T. olive oil
1 T. butter
2 2-lb. butternut squash, peeled and cubed
1 onion, chopped
1 clove garlic, minced
1/2 t. allspice
2 14 1/2-oz. cans chicken broth
Garnish: sour cream, allspice

Combine oil and butter in a large saucepan over medium heat. Add squash, onion and garlic. Cook for about 5 minutes, stirring occasionally, until crisp-tender. Add allspice; cook just a minute more. Add broth. Bring to a boil; cover. Reduce heat to low; simmer for 15 minutes or until squash is tender. Process in a food processor until smooth. Return to saucepan; heat until hot. If a thinner soup is preferred, add a little more broth or water. Ladle soup into soup bowls. Garnish, if desired. Serve with crackers. Serves 8.

Teri Johnson
North Ogden, UT

LIGHT THE CANDLES and WELCOME YOUR GUESTS!

If you like treats with plenty of zip, serve Peppery Molasses Cookies with Spiced Chocolate Coffee. On the traditional side, the fudgy goodness of Chocolate Chess Pie is sweet to savor!

Peppery Molasses Cookies

These are really spicy…the black pepper gives them a kick!

³/₄ c. butter, softened
³/₄ c. sugar
1 egg
¹/₄ c. molasses
2 c. all-purpose flour
2 t. baking soda
1¹/₂ t. pepper
1 t. cinnamon
¹/₂ t. salt
additional sugar

Beat butter and sugar in a large bowl until fluffy. Beat in egg; add molasses. Combine flour and next 4 ingredients. Gradually add to butter mixture; mix well. Form into one-inch balls and roll in sugar. Arrange 2 inches apart on ungreased baking sheets. Bake at 350 degrees for 12 to 15 minutes. Remove and cool on wire racks. Makes 3¹/₂ to 4 dozen.

Lisa Ashton
Aston, PA

Peppery Molasses Cookies
Spiced Chocolate Coffee

Brandied Cranberries

Family & friends look forward to this spirited cranberry relish at our holiday dinners.

2 c. sugar
12-oz. pkg. cranberries
¹/₂ c. brandy

Combine all ingredients in a lightly greased 1¹/₂-quart casserole dish. Cover and bake at 300 degrees for 45 minutes, stirring several times while baking. Refrigerate overnight; serve warm or cold. Serves 5.

Robin Dennis
Vernonia, OR

Spiced Chocolate Coffee

Top with sweetened whipped cream for a special treat.

8 c. brewed coffee
¹/₃ c. sugar
¹/₄ c. chocolate syrup
4 4-inch cinnamon sticks, broken
1¹/₂ t. whole cloves
Garnish: cinnamon sticks, sweetened whipped cream

Combine first 3 ingredients in a slow cooker; set aside. Wrap spices in a coffee filter or cheesecloth and tie with kitchen string; add to slow cooker. Cover and cook on low setting for 2 to 3 hours. Remove and discard spices. Ladle coffee into mugs. Garnish, if desired. Makes 8¹/₄ cups.

Regina Vining
Warwick, RI

A TINY TREAT TO TAKE HOME

good cheer

Chocolate Chess Pie

My favorite winter recipe...Mom always made it at Christmas.

$^1/_2$ c. butter
$1^1/_2$ 1-oz. sqs. unsweetened baking chocolate, chopped
1 c. brown sugar, packed
$^1/_2$ c. sugar
2 eggs, beaten
1 T. milk
1 t. all-purpose flour
1 t. vanilla extract
9-inch pie crust
Garnish: whipped cream

Melt butter and chocolate in a small saucepan over low heat; set aside. Combine sugars, eggs, milk, flour and vanilla in a medium bowl. Gradually add chocolate mixture, beating constantly. Pour into unbaked pie crust; bake at 325 degrees for 40 to 45 minutes. Let cool before serving. Garnish, if desired. Serves 6 to 8.

Heidi Jo McManaman
Grand Rapids, MI

Apple Gingerbread Cobbler

My new favorite dessert...the flavors are scrumptious!

14-oz. pkg. gingerbread cake mix, divided
$^3/_4$ c. water
$^1/_4$ c. brown sugar, packed
$^1/_2$ c. butter, softened and divided
$^1/_2$ c. chopped pecans
2 21-oz. cans apple pie filling
Optional: vanilla ice cream

Mix together 2 cups gingerbread cake mix and water until smooth; set aside.

Stir together remaining gingerbread cake mix and brown sugar; cut in $^1/_4$ cup butter until mixture is crumbly. Stir in pecans; set aside.

Combine pie filling and remaining $^1/_4$ cup butter in a large saucepan; cook, stirring often, for 5 minutes over medium heat or until thoroughly heated. Spoon apple mixture evenly into a lightly greased 11"x7" baking pan. Spoon gingerbread mixture over apple mixture; sprinkle with pecan mixture. Bake at 375 degrees for 30 to 35 minutes or until set. Serve with scoops of ice cream, if desired. Serves 8.

Wendy Jacobs
Idaho Falls, ID

Chocolate Chess Pie

A very merry BRUNCH!

It's time to rise and shine, because Christmas Day is here! All the fun around the tree can really boost appetites, so planning a quick-to-fix breakfast is important. These yummy recipes will help you put a sweet or savory meal on the table in a hurry. Several dishes can be prepared and refrigerated the night before, so all you have to do is bake them the next day! You won't have to miss a moment of your family's time together.

Gingerbread Pancakes

Gingerbread Pancakes

Oh-so scrumptious topped with tangy Lemon Sauce.

1½ c. all-purpose flour
1 t. baking powder
¼ t. baking soda
¼ t. salt
1 t. cinnamon
½ t. ground ginger
1 egg
1¼ c. milk
¼ c. molasses
3 T. oil
Garnish: lemon zest strips

Sift together first 6 ingredients in a medium bowl; set aside. In a large bowl, beat egg and milk until well blended; stir in molasses and oil. Add flour mixture to milk mixture, stirring just until moistened. Pour batter by ⅓ cupfuls onto a lightly greased hot griddle. Cook over medium heat until bubbly on top; flip and continue to cook until golden. Serve with lemon sauce. Garnish, if desired. Serves 4.

Lemon Sauce:
½ c. sugar
1 T. cornstarch
⅛ t. nutmeg
1 c. water
2 T. butter
½ t. lemon zest
2 T. lemon juice

Stir together sugar, cornstarch and nutmeg in a small saucepan; add water. Cook over medium heat until thick and bubbly; cook and stir for an additional 2 minutes. Remove from heat; add remaining ingredients. Stir just until butter melts. Serve warm.

Kendall Hale
Lynn, MA

Holiday Morning French Toast or Tangy Cranberry Breakfast Cake will energize your family for a day filled with festivities!

Holiday Morning French Toast

A sweet breakfast treat that's sure to have family & friends asking for the recipe.

1 c. brown sugar, packed
1/2 c. butter, melted
1 T. cinnamon, divided
3 to 4 Granny Smith apples, peeled, cored and thinly sliced
1/2 c. raisins
1 loaf French or Italian bread, sliced 1-inch thick
8 to 9 eggs
2 c. milk
1 T. vanilla extract
Optional: syrup

Combine brown sugar, butter and one teaspoon cinnamon in a lightly greased 13"x9" baking pan. Add apples and raisins; toss to coat well. Spread apple mixture evenly over bottom of baking pan. Arrange slices of bread on top; set aside. Blend together eggs, milk, vanilla and remaining 2 teaspoons cinnamon until well mixed. Pour mixture over bread, soaking bread completely. Cover with aluminum foil and refrigerate for 4 to 24 hours.

Bake, covered, at 375 degrees for 40 minutes. Uncover and bake an additional 15 minutes. Let stand 5 minutes. Serve warm with syrup, if desired. Makes 12 servings.

Coleen Lambert
Casco, WI

Sausage & Cheddar Grits

A rich, savory version of a southern favorite...yum!

4 eggs, beaten
4 c. water
1 t. salt
1 c. quick-cooking grits, uncooked
1 lb. ground pork sausage, browned and drained
1 1/2 c. shredded Cheddar cheese, divided
1 c. milk
1/4 c. butter

Place eggs in a small bowl; set aside. Bring water and salt to a boil in large saucepan over medium heat. Stir in grits; cook for 4 to 5 minutes. Remove from heat. Stir a small amount of hot grits mixture into eggs; stir egg mixture back into saucepan. Add sausage, one cup cheese, milk and butter; blend together well. Pour into a greased 13"x9" baking pan. Sprinkle with remaining 1/2 cup cheese. Bake, uncovered, at 350 degrees for one hour or until cheese is golden. If cheese is getting golden early, cover with aluminum foil. Let cool for about 10 minutes before serving. Serves 6 to 8.

Sharon Brown
Orange Park, FL

Christmas Morning Muffins

To save time, pour batter into muffin tins the night before, cover with a damp towel and refrigerate until ready to bake.

2 eggs, beaten
3/4 c. milk
1/2 c. oil
2 c. all-purpose flour
1/3 c. sugar
3 t. baking powder
1 t. salt

Blend eggs, milk and oil together; add remaining ingredients, stirring until just moistened. Fill paper-lined or lightly greased muffin cups 2/3 full; bake at 400 degrees for 20 minutes or until golden. Remove from pan; spread topping on while warm. Serve at once. Makes 12.

Topping:
1 c. sugar
1/2 c. butter, melted
2 t. cinnamon

Combine all ingredients; whisk until creamy.

Mary Jones
North Lawrence, OH

Tangy Cranberry Breakfast Cake

Three heavenly layers!

2 c. all-purpose flour
1 1/3 c. sugar, divided
1 1/2 t. baking powder
1/2 t. baking soda
1/4 t. salt
2 eggs, divided
3/4 c. orange juice
1/4 c. butter, melted
2 t. vanilla extract, divided
2 c. cranberries, coarsely chopped
Optional: 1 T. orange zest
8-oz. pkg. cream cheese, softened

Combine flour, one cup sugar, baking powder, baking soda and salt in a large bowl; mix well and set aside. Combine one egg, orange juice, butter and one teaspoon vanilla in a small bowl; mix well and stir into flour mixture until well combined. Fold in cranberries and zest, if using. Pour into a greased 9" round springform pan and set aside.

Beat together cream cheese and remaining 1/3 cup sugar in a small bowl until smooth. Add remaining egg and one teaspoon vanilla; mix well. Spread over batter; sprinkle with topping. Place pan on a baking sheet; bake at 350 degrees for 1 1/4 hours or until golden. Let cool on wire rack for 15 minutes before removing sides of pan. Serves 12.

Topping:
6 T. all-purpose flour
1/4 c. sugar
2 T. butter

Combine flour and sugar in a small bowl. Cut in butter with a fork until mixture resembles coarse crumbs.

Linda Hendrix
Moundville, MO

Tangy Cranberry Breakfast Cake

Jumbo Quiche Muffins

Whether you make Jumbo Quiche Muffins or Mini Spinach & Bacon Quiches, you can be sure every bite will disappear! Don't be surprised if your family requests Company Breakfast Casserole again next year.

Mini Spinach & Bacon Quiches

Mini Spinach & Bacon Quiches

An elegant addition to a holiday brunch buffet that can be assembled the night before and refrigerated.

1/4 c. onion, diced
3 slices bacon, crisply cooked and crumbled, drippings reserved
10-oz. pkg. frozen chopped spinach, thawed and drained
1/8 t. salt
1/2 t. pepper
1/8 t. nutmeg
15-oz. container ricotta cheese
8-oz. pkg. shredded mozzarella cheese
1 c. grated Parmesan cheese
3 eggs, beaten

In a skillet over medium heat, cook onion in reserved drippings until tender. Add spinach and seasonings; stir over medium heat about 3 minutes or until liquid evaporates. Remove from heat; stir in bacon and cool.

Combine cheeses in a large bowl. Add eggs; stir until well blended. Add cooled spinach mixture; stir until well blended. Divide mixture evenly among 12 lightly greased muffin cups. Bake at 350 degrees for 40 minutes or until filling is set. Let stand 10 minutes; run a thin knife around edges to release. Serve warm. Makes 12.

Vickie

Jumbo Quiche Muffins

These oversized muffins are always a breakfast hit.

16.3-oz. tube refrigerated flaky
    buttermilk biscuits
1/2 c. cream cheese, softened
4 eggs, beaten
1/4 t. seasoned salt
1/4 t. pepper
6 slices bacon, crisply cooked
    and crumbled
1/2 c. shredded Cheddar cheese

Place each biscuit into a greased jumbo muffin cup; press to form a well. Combine cream cheese, eggs, salt and pepper. Spoon 3 tablespoons egg mixture into each biscuit well; sprinkle with bacon and top with cheese. Bake at 375 degrees for 15 minutes. Serves 8.

Debra Alf
Robbinsdale, MN

Ham, Cheddar & Chive Wraps

I love these handy wraps...they're so easy to make and as yummy as a classic ham & cheese omelet.

1 T. butter
4 eggs, beaten
1 1/4 c. cooked ham, diced
1/2 c. Cheddar cheese, cubed
2 T. fresh chives, snipped
pepper to taste
4 flour tortillas, warmed

Melt butter in a medium skillet; pour in eggs. Add remaining ingredients except tortillas. Scramble until eggs are desired consistency; remove from heat. Place egg mixture in tortillas and wrap tightly. Secure with toothpicks and serve warm. Makes 4.

Jackie Smulski
Lyons, IL

Company Breakfast Casserole

Company Breakfast Casserole

For a southwest flair, replace the mushrooms with a small can of sliced olives, add Monterey Jack cheese instead of Cheddar and serve with spicy salsa on the side.

16-oz. pkg. shredded frozen
    hashbrowns, thawed and
    divided
1 onion, chopped and divided
1 lb. ground pork sausage, browned
    and drained
1 green pepper, chopped
4-oz. can sliced mushrooms,
    drained
1/2 to 1 c. shredded Cheddar cheese,
    divided
1 doz. eggs, beaten
1 1/2 c. milk
salt and pepper to taste
Optional: garlic salt to taste

Spread half of the hashbrowns in a lightly greased 13"x9" baking pan. Layer ingredients as follows: half the onion, sausage, remaining onion, green pepper, mushrooms and half the cheese. In a separate bowl, whisk together eggs, milk and seasonings. Pour egg mixture over casserole; top with remaining hashbrowns and remaining cheese. Cover with aluminum foil and refrigerate overnight.

Bake, covered, at 350 degrees for 45 to 60 minutes. Uncover and bake an additional 20 minutes or until a knife inserted in center comes out clean. Serves 8 to 10.

Jena Buckler
Bloomington Springs, TN

All the Sweetness of the Season

It's the season when baked goods fill every kitchen with their sweetness! Mary Elizabeth plans to surprise her friend Kate with a rich Chocolate-Cappuccino Cheesecake, while Holly makes colorful Sugar Cookie Pops for all her nieces and nephews. Kate thinks Christmas Cherry-Berry Pie is a perfect potluck dessert. Or maybe she'll make a Red Velvet Cake with a very special fluffy frosting!

Chocolate-Cappuccino Cheesecake

This makes an absolutely delicious gift...if you can bear to give it away!

1¹/₂ c. pecans, finely chopped
1¹/₂ c. chocolate wafer cookies, crushed
¹/₃ c. butter, melted
¹/₂ c. semi-sweet chocolate chips, melted

Mix pecans, cookies and butter together; press into the bottom and up the sides of a greased 9" springform pan. Drizzle with chocolate; chill until chocolate is firm.

Pour filling into crust; bake at 300 degrees for one hour and 10 minutes. Cool completely. Cover and chill 8 hours. Spread topping over cake. Remove sides of pan. Makes 12 servings.

Filling:
2 8-oz. pkgs. cream cheese, softened
1¹/₂ c. semi-sweet chocolate chips, melted and cooled
1 c. brown sugar, packed
4 eggs
1 c. sour cream
¹/₃ c. cold coffee
2 t. vanilla extract

Combine all ingredients; blend until smooth.

Topping:
²/₃ c. whipping cream
¹/₄ c. sugar
¹/₂ c. semi-sweet chocolate chips

Heat whipping cream and sugar over low heat, whisking constantly. Add chocolate chips, whisking until smooth.

Sandy Stacy
Medway, OH

Chocolate-Cappuccino Cheesecake

Red Velvet Cake

My grandma and aunt make this wonderful cake for my birthday and again for Christmas. The homemade frosting is scrumptious...well worth the time!

18¼-oz. pkg. fudge marble cake
    mix
1 t. baking soda
1½ c. buttermilk
2 eggs, beaten
1-oz. bottle red food coloring
1 t. vanilla extract

Combine dry cake mix, fudge marble packet and baking soda in a medium bowl; add remaining ingredients. Blend with an electric mixer on low speed until moistened. Beat on high speed for 2 minutes. Pour batter into 2 greased and floured 9" round cake pans. Bake at 350 degrees for 30 to 35 minutes or until cake tests done. Cool in pans for 10 minutes; turn out onto a wire rack. Cool completely; if desired, freeze layers overnight to make cake easier to frost. Spread vanilla frosting between layers and on top and sides of cake. Makes 10 to 12 servings.

Vanilla Frosting:
5 T. all-purpose flour
1 c. milk
1 c. butter, softened
1 c. sugar
2 t. vanilla extract

Whisk flour and milk in a saucepan over medium-low heat until smooth. Bring to a boil; cook and stir for 2 minutes or until thickened. Cover and refrigerate until chilled.

In a medium bowl, blend butter and sugar; add chilled milk mixture. Beat for 8 minutes or until fluffy; stir in vanilla.

Angela Miller
Jefferson City, MO

The richness of Red Velvet Cake will become a delicious tradition at your house! For the young and young at heart, make Chocolate & Marshmallow Cupcakes or Chocolate-Covered Cherry Cups.

Red Velvet Cake

Chocolate & Marshmallow Cupcakes

Super for the kids' Christmas parties!

8-oz. pkg. unsweetened dark
    baking chocolate, chopped
1 c. butter, softened
4 eggs
1 c. sugar
¾ c. all-purpose flour
1 t. salt
½ c. mini semi-sweet chocolate
    chips
Garnish: ½ c. mini marshmallows

Place chocolate and butter together in a microwave-safe bowl; heat on high setting just until melted. Cool until just warm. Blend together eggs and sugar until light and foamy. Add flour and salt; mix well. Pour in chocolate mixture; blend until smooth. Spoon batter into 12 paper-lined muffin cups; sprinkle chocolate chips evenly over tops.

Bake at 350 degrees for 15 minutes or until toothpick tests clean. Remove from oven; arrange several marshmallows on top of each cupcake. Broil just until marshmallows turn golden. Remove from oven and let stand 5 minutes to cool slightly. Makes one dozen.

Kathy Grashoff
Fort Wayne, IN

Chocolate-Covered Cherry Cups

I created this simpler version of a more difficult recipe and I think they are wonderful. My grandchildren like to push the cherries in for me.

20-oz. pkg. brownie mix
16-oz. jar maraschino cherries, drained,
   $\frac{1}{2}$ c. juice reserved and divided
6-oz. pkg. semi-sweet chocolate chips
$\frac{1}{2}$ c. sweetened condensed milk

Prepare brownie mix according to package directions, using $\frac{1}{4}$ cup cherry juice plus water needed to equal amount of water called for in directions. Place paper liners in mini muffin cups; fill about $\frac{1}{2}$ full of brownie batter. Push a cherry into each cup; bake at 350 degrees for 15 to 20 minutes. Remove baked cups in liners from muffin cups; let cool.

Combine chocolate chips and condensed milk in a small saucepan; stir over low heat until melted. Remove from heat; stir in remaining $\frac{1}{4}$ cup cherry juice as needed for frosting consistency. Place a dollop of warm frosting on each cherry cup; let cool. Makes 3 dozen.

Robin Healy
Honeoye, NY

Chocolate & Marshmallow Cupcakes

Chocolate-Covered Cherry Cups

Melt-in-your-mouth Candy Cane Puffs and a sweet/tart pie...these flavors of Christmas are absolutely scrumptious!

Frosted Mocha Brownies

You'll never go back to brownies from a mix after you've tasted these yummy chocolate-frosted brownies.

1 c. sugar
1/2 c. plus 3 T. butter, softened and divided
1/3 c. plus 1/4 c. baking cocoa, divided
1 t. instant coffee granules
2 eggs, beaten
1 1/2 t. vanilla extract, divided
2/3 c. all-purpose flour
1/2 t. baking powder
1/4 t. salt
1/2 c. chopped walnuts
2 c. powdered sugar, divided
2 to 3 T. milk

Combine sugar, 1/2 cup butter, 1/3 cup baking cocoa and coffee granules in a medium saucepan. Cook and stir over medium heat until butter is melted. Remove from heat; cool for 5 minutes. Add eggs and one teaspoon vanilla; mix just until combined. Stir in flour, baking powder and salt; add nuts. Spread batter in a greased 9"x9" baking pan. Bake at 350 degrees for 25 minutes or until set. Cool in pan on a wire rack.

Beat remaining 3 tablespoons butter until light and fluffy; add remaining 1/4 cup cocoa. Gradually add one cup powdered sugar, mixing well. Stir in 2 tablespoons milk and remaining 1/2 teaspoon vanilla. Gradually stir in remaining one cup powdered sugar and additional milk as needed to make a spreading consistency. Spread over cooled brownies; slice into bars. Makes one dozen.

Connie Bryant
Topeka, KS

Candy Cane Puffs

Just right for giving, these look so pretty in a Christmas tin.

2 1/2 c. all-purpose flour
1/4 t. salt
1/2 c. butter, softened
1 c. powdered sugar
1 egg
1 t. vanilla extract
1/2 t. peppermint extract
8-oz. pkg. white chocolate chips
1/2 c. peppermint candies, crushed

Combine flour and salt; set aside.
Blend together butter and sugar; beat in egg and extracts. Mix into flour mixture using low speed. Wrap dough in plastic wrap; refrigerate for one hour.
Shape dough into walnut-size balls; place on lightly greased baking sheets. Bake at 375 degrees for 10 to 12 minutes; cool. Melt white chocolate chips in a double boiler; dip cooled cookies into melted chocolate. Roll in crushed peppermint candy; set on wax paper until hardened. Makes about 4 dozen.

Kristine Marumoto
Sandy, UT

Candy Cane Puffs

Christmas Cherry-Berry Pie

The cranberry sauce adds a special flavor to the all-time favorite cherry pie.

21-oz. can cherry pie filling
16-oz. can whole-berry cranberry
    sauce
1/4 c. sugar
3 T. quick-cooking tapioca,
    uncooked
1 t. lemon juice
1/4 t. cinnamon
2 T. butter
2 T. milk

Combine all ingredients except butter and milk; let stand 15 minutes. Divide pastry in half; set one half aside. Roll half the dough out and line a 9" pie plate; add filling mixture. Dot with butter. Roll remaining dough into a 12-inch circle; cut into 3/4-inch wide strips. Lay strips on pie at one-inch intervals; fold back alternate strips as you weave crosswise strips over and under. Trim crust even with outer rim of pie plate. Dampen edge of crust with water; fold over strips, seal and crimp. Brush lattice with milk. Bake at 400 degrees for 40 to 45 minutes, covering edge of crust with aluminum foil after 15 minutes to prevent browning. Serves 8.

Flaky Pastry:
3 c. all-purpose flour
1 c. plus 1 T. shortening
1/3 c. cold water
1 egg, beaten
1 T. vinegar
1/2 t. salt

Blend together flour and shortening. Add remaining ingredients; blend with an electric mixer on low speed.

Joyce LaMure
Reno, NV

Christmas Cherry-Berry Pie

Sugar Cookie Pops

(Shown on front cover.)
You'll want to buy several containers of colored sugars and jimmies so you'll have plenty for coating these cookie balls.

1/2 c. butter, softened
1/2 c. shortening
1 c. sugar
1 c. powdered sugar
2 eggs
3/4 c. vegetable oil
2 t. vanilla extract
4 c. all-purpose flour
1 t. baking soda
1 t. salt
1 t. cream of tartar
Colored sugars, sparkling sugars
    and multicolored jimmies
4" white lollipop sticks

Beat butter and shortening at medium speed with an electric mixer until fluffy; add sugars, beating well. Add eggs, oil and vanilla, beating until blended.

Combine flour and next 3 ingredients; add to butter mixture, blending well. Cover and chill dough 2 hours or overnight.

Shape dough into 1 1/2-inch balls. Roll each ball in colored sugar or jimmies in individual bowls, pressing gently, if necessary, to coat balls. Place 2 inches apart on ungreased baking sheets. Insert sticks about one inch into each cookie to resemble a lollipop.

Bake at 350 degrees for 10 to 11 minutes or until set. Let cool 2 minutes on baking sheets; remove cookie pops to wire racks to cool completely. Makes 4 1/2 dozen.

OH, slow good!

While you shop for presents or decorate the tree, it's so nice to be able to rely on your slow cooker. The yummiest entrées, side dishes and desserts can bubble and simmer for hours! When it's time to prepare Christmas dinner, you'll save space in the oven by making Crockery Sage Dressing. And who can resist Slow-Cooked Brown Sugar Apples? They'll fill your house with a heavenly cinnamon fragrance!

Slow-Cooked Brown Sugar Apples

Slow-Cooked Brown Sugar Apples

Nothing says comfort like the aroma of these apples cooking…unless, of course, it's sitting down to enjoy them.

6 apples, cored
3/4 c. orange juice
1/2 c. apple cider
1/2 c. brown sugar, packed
1/4 t. cinnamon
Optional: frozen whipped topping, thawed

Peel a strip around the top of each apple to help prevent cracking. Arrange apples in a slow cooker. In a large bowl, combine remaining ingredients except whipped topping; mix to blend. Spoon over apples. Cover and cook on low setting for 3 to 4 hours or until apples are tender. Cool slightly and serve warm with whipped topping, if desired. Makes 6 servings.

Lynn Williams
Muncie, IN

Slow-Cooker Lasagna

Use a mixture of ground beef and ground Italian sausage if you like.

1 lb. ground beef
1 c. onion, chopped
2 cloves garlic, minced
29-oz. can tomato sauce
6-oz. can tomato paste
1 c. water
1 t. salt
1 t. dried oregano
16-oz. pkg. shredded mozzarella cheese
16-oz. container cottage cheese
½ c. grated Parmesan cheese
10 lasagna noodles, uncooked

Brown beef, onion and garlic in a large skillet; drain. Add tomato sauce, tomato paste, water, salt and oregano; set aside.

In a medium bowl, stir together cheeses. Layer ⅓ meat sauce, ½ uncooked lasagna noodles (broken to fit slow cooker) and ½ cheese mixture in a slow cooker. Repeat layers, finishing with meat sauce. Cover and cook on low setting for 4 to 5 hours. Serves 6 to 8.

Maria Benedict
Stowe, PA

Spoon Bread Florentine

Deliciously different and so simple to make.

10-oz. pkg. frozen chopped spinach,
   thawed and drained
6 green onions, sliced
1 red pepper, chopped
6-oz. pkg. cornbread mix
4 eggs, beaten
½ c. butter, melted
1 c. cottage cheese
1¼ t. seasoned salt

Combine all ingredients in a large bowl; mix well. Spoon into a lightly greased slow cooker. Cover and cook on low setting 4 to 5 hours or on high setting for 2 to 3 hours. Cook until edges are golden and a knife tip inserted in center comes out clean. Makes 10 servings.

Jo Ann

Enjoy the comfort of a home-cooked recipe like Slow-Cooker Lasagna or Down-on-the-Bayou Gumbo, even when you don't have a lot of time to spend in the kitchen! Top off a friends & family evening with Hot Fudge Spoon Cake. It's a rich and satisfying treat!

Crockery Sage Dressing

How clever! Make dressing in your slow cooker and free up the oven for other holiday dishes.

2 c. onion, chopped
2 c. celery, chopped
1 c. butter
2 loaves white bread, torn
1½ t. dried sage
1½ t. salt
1 t. poultry seasoning
½ t. dried thyme
½ t. dried marjoram
½ t. pepper
14-oz. can chicken broth
2 eggs, beaten

Sauté onion and celery in butter in a skillet; set aside.

Place bread in a large mixing bowl; add seasonings and toss well. Add onion mixture and enough broth to moisten bread; toss well. Stir in eggs and mix well. Spoon into a slow cooker. Cook, covered, on low setting for 4 to 5 hours, stirring occasionally and adding more broth as needed. Serves 10 to 12.

Gina Rongved-Van Wyk
Rapid City, SD

Slow-Cooker Lasagna

Down-on-the-Bayou Gumbo

You can't help but smile with a bowl of gumbo in front of you!

3 T. all-purpose flour
3 T. oil
1/2 lb. smoked sausage, sliced 1/2-inch thick
2 c. frozen okra
14 1/2-oz. can diced tomatoes
1 onion, chopped
1 green pepper, chopped
3 cloves garlic, minced
1/4 t. cayenne pepper
3/4 lb. cooked medium shrimp, peeled
1 1/2 c. long-cooking rice, cooked

Stir together flour and oil in a small saucepan over medium heat. Cook, stirring constantly, for 5 minutes. Reduce heat and cook, stirring constantly, for about 10 minutes or until mixture turns reddish brown. Spoon mixture into a slow cooker; stir in remaining ingredients except shrimp and rice. Cover and cook on high setting for one hour; then 5 hours on low setting. Twenty minutes before serving, add shrimp to slow cooker; mix well. Cover and cook on low setting. Ladle gumbo over cooked rice in soup bowls. Makes 6 servings.

Sue Neely
Greenville, IL

Hot Fudge Spoon Cake

Down-on-the-Bayou Gumbo

Hot Fudge Spoon Cake

Heavenly!

1 c. all-purpose flour
1 3/4 c. brown sugar,
 packed and divided
1/4 c. plus 3 T. baking cocoa,
 divided
2 t. baking powder
1/4 t. salt
1/2 c. milk
2 T. butter, melted
1/2 t. vanilla extract
1 3/4 c. hot water
Optional: vanilla ice cream

Combine flour, one cup brown sugar, 3 tablespoons cocoa, baking powder and salt in a medium bowl. Whisk in milk, butter and vanilla. Spread evenly in a slow cooker. Mix together remaining 3/4 cup brown sugar and 1/4 cup cocoa; sprinkle evenly over top of batter. Pour in hot water; do not stir. Cover and cook on high setting for 2 hours or until a toothpick inserted one inch deep comes out clean. Spoon warm cake into bowls; top with vanilla ice cream, if desired. Makes 6 servings.

Sara Plott
Monument, CO

The More Cooks, the Merrier!

Here's a fun way to save time this holiday season…get your friends involved in a supper swap! When three or four families take turns cooking dinner, everyone gets a few nights a week without kitchen duty. Each household cooks one big meal and shares it with the other families. All you have to do is get together to plan the week's menu, cook once, and you're done! These recipes can be adjusted, depending on the number of servings you need. If you like, add other side dishes and desserts to round out your meals.

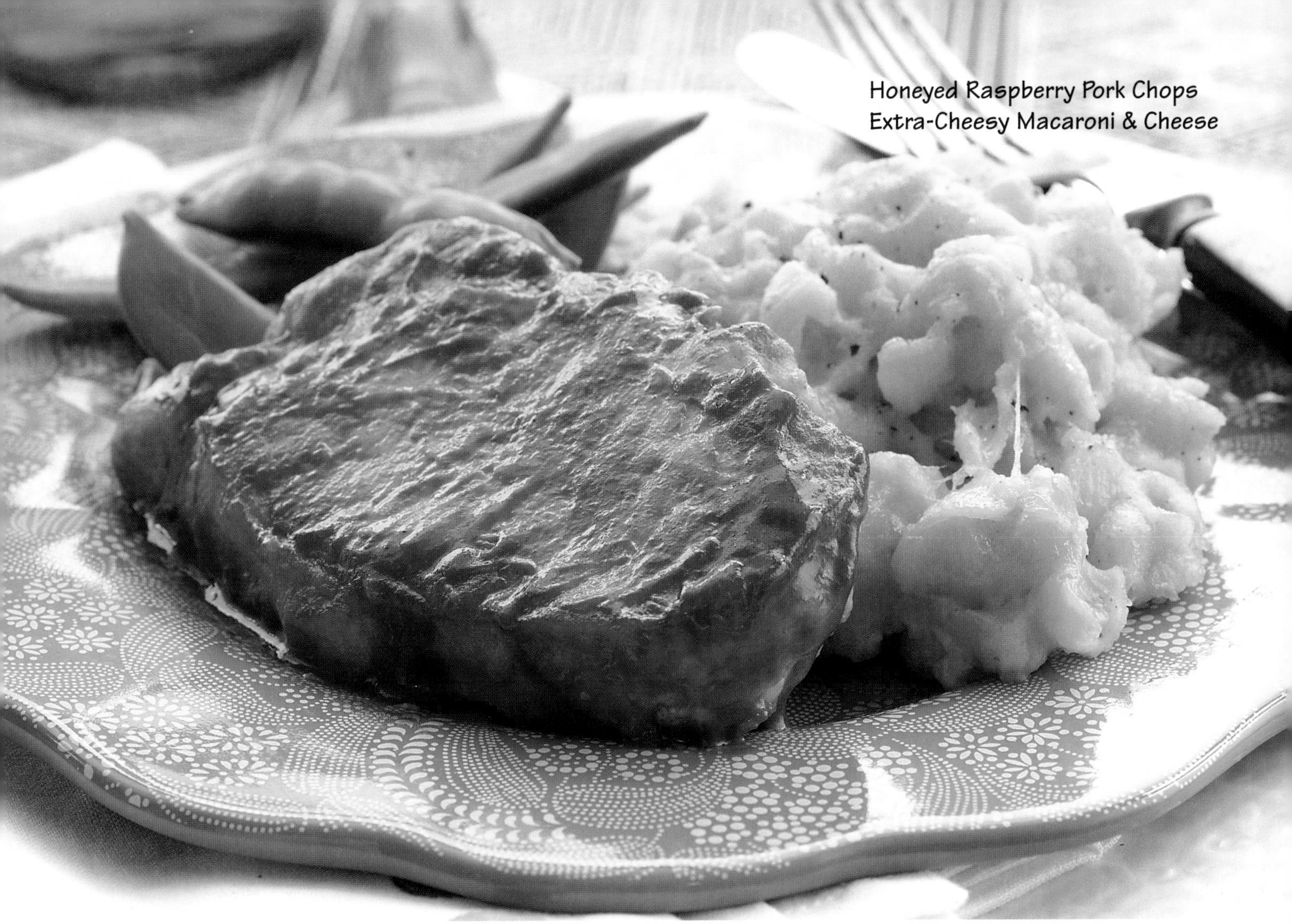

Honeyed Raspberry Pork Chops
Extra-Cheesy Macaroni & Cheese

Honeyed Raspberry Pork Chops

Raspberry jam pairs up with honey mustard to make a flavorful sauce.

4 boneless pork chops
2 T. all-purpose flour
1/3 c. honey mustard
1/4 c. raspberry jam
2 T. cider vinegar
1 T. olive oil

Dredge pork chops in flour, shaking off any excess. In a small bowl, combine honey mustard, jam and vinegar; set aside.

Heat oil in a large skillet over medium heat. Add pork chops and sauté until golden on both sides. Stir in honey mustard mixture; bring to a boil. Reduce heat and simmer for 10 minutes or until chops are no longer pink inside. Serves 4.

Elaine Slabinski
Monroe Township, NJ

Extra-Cheesy Macaroni & Cheese

My husband says this is the best macaroni and cheese he's ever eaten!

8-oz. pkg. shredded Italian-blend cheese
8-oz. pkg. shredded sharp Cheddar cheese
2 eggs, beaten
12-oz. can evaporated milk
1 1/2 c. milk
1 t. salt
3/4 t. dry mustard
1/2 t. pepper
1/4 t. cayenne pepper
8-oz. pkg. small shell macaroni, uncooked

Combine cheeses in a large bowl; set aside.

Whisk together eggs and next 6 ingredients in a large bowl; stir in macaroni and 3 cups cheese mixture. Pour macaroni mixture into a slow cooker; sprinkle with 3/4 cup cheese mixture. Cover and cook on low setting for 4 hours.

Sprinkle servings with remaining cheese mixture. Serves 6 to 8.

Valarie Dennard
Palatka, FL

For a farmhouse style dinner, layer a slice of Texas toast with Make-Ahead Mashed Potatoes and hearty Pepper-Crusted Roast Beef. Or, you can warm up a wintry evening with Snowy Day Chili and Broccoli-Cheese Cornbread.

Pepper-Crusted Roast Beef
Make-Ahead Mashed Potatoes

Pepper-Crusted Roast Beef

A caramelized brown sugar sauce is spooned over tender slices of beef.

2 to 3-lb. boneless beef rib
　　roast
1/4 c. garlic, minced
3 T. peppercorns
1/4 c. Worcestershire sauce
2 red onions, thinly sliced
1 T. oil
1 T. brown sugar, packed
2 T. balsamic vinegar

Rub roast with garlic and coat fat side of roast with peppercorns. Drizzle with Worcestershire sauce. Place in a roaster pan. Roast at 350 degrees for 40 minutes to one hour or until meat thermometer reaches 150 degrees; keep warm.

Cook onions in oil in a small skillet over medium heat until onions are soft. Add brown sugar and vinegar; cook until caramelized, about 8 to 10 minutes.

Slice roast; serve onions over top. Serves 6 to 8.

Linda Behling
Cecil, PA

Make-Ahead Mashed Potatoes

It's impossible not to love the homestyle flavor of these potatoes.

6 to 8 potatoes, peeled and quartered
1/4 c. butter, softened
8-oz. pkg. cream cheese, softened

Boil potatoes until tender; drain. Combine potatoes, butter and cream cheese in a large bowl; let stand 10 minutes or until cream cheese melts. Mash until smooth. Refrigerate until serving time; reheat in a microwave. Serves 6.

Mary Brown
Sayre, PA

BE PREPARED.

Monday
Tuesday
Wednes
Thursday
Friday
Saturday
Sunday

Broccoli-Cheese Cornbread

This recipe, given to me by my Aunt Ora Lee, is one I enjoy toting to potluck dinners at church and at work.

2 8½-oz. pkgs. cornbread mix
1½ c. cottage cheese
5 eggs, beaten
10-oz. pkg. frozen chopped broccoli,
    thawed
1 onion, chopped
½ c. margarine, melted
1 c. shredded Cheddar cheese

Mix together all ingredients except Cheddar cheese; spread in a lightly greased 13"x9" baking pan. Bake, uncovered, at 350 degrees for 45 minutes. Sprinkle with cheese and bake for an additional 3 minutes or until cheese is melted. Makes about 12 servings.

Jane Reynolds
Rowlett, TX

In this World, We must HELP one Another.
• JEAN de LA FONTAINE •

Broccoli-Cheese Cornbread
Snowy Day Chili

Snowy Day Chili

In Wisconsin snow is inevitable, but shoveling sidewalks isn't so dreaded when there's a pot of chili simmering on the stove!

2 lbs. ground beef or venison
2 c. chopped onion
4 c. canned or homemade
    tomato sauce
4 c. water
15-oz. can kidney beans,
    drained and rinsed
6-oz. can tomato paste
¼ c. Worcestershire sauce
2 T. brown sugar, packed
1 T. seasoned salt
1 T. lemon juice
3 bay leaves
chili powder to taste
Optional: hot pepper sauce to
    taste
Garnish: shredded Cheddar
    cheese, chopped onion,
    sour cream, corn chips

In a large stockpot over medium heat, brown meat; drain. Stir in remaining ingredients except garnish. Reduce heat; simmer for 3 to 4 hours, stirring occasionally.

Garnish if desired. Makes 8 to 10 servings.

Kathie Poritz
Burlington, WI

Add a little zip to your meal with Guacamole Salad and Slow-Cooker Roast for Tacos. For dessert, Caramel-Coffee Tassies are the perfect after-dinner bites of sweetness.

Guacamole Salad

Serve as a salad or an appetizer with corn chips or croutons.

2 avocados, peeled, pitted and chopped
1 tomato, chopped
1 cucumber, peeled and chopped
2 green onions, chopped
2 T. lime juice
1 clove garlic, minced
1 T. dried parsley
³/₄ t. salt
¹/₂ t. pepper
¹/₄ t. garlic powder
hot pepper sauce to taste

Toss all ingredients together gently; cover and refrigerate until ready to serve. Serves 4.

Michael Curry
Ardmore, OK

Slow-Cooker Roast for Tacos

Don't forget to offer all the tasty taco toppers...shredded cheese, sour cream, lettuce, tomatoes, onions and salsa. Olé!

4 to 5-lb. beef chuck roast
1 T. chili powder
1 t. ground cumin
1 t. onion powder
1 t. garlic powder
2 14¹/₂-oz. cans Mexican-style stewed tomatoes
taco shells

Place roast in a large slow cooker; sprinkle with spices. Add tomatoes with juice around the roast. Cover and cook on low setting for 8 to 10 hours.

Using 2 forks, shred roast and spoon into taco shells. Makes 10 cups.

Dana Thompson
Gooseberry Patch

Guacamole Salad
Slow-Cooker Roast for Tacos

Caramel-Coffee Tassies

In a word...delectable!

1/2 c. butter, softened
3-oz. pkg. cream cheese, softened
1 c. all-purpose flour
14-oz. pkg. caramels, unwrapped
1/4 c. evaporated milk
1 1/2 t. coffee liqueur or brewed coffee

Beat butter and cream cheese together until well blended; stir in flour. Form into a ball; chill for one hour or overnight.

Shape dough into 1/2-inch balls; press each into an ungreased mini muffin cup. Bake at 350 degrees for 10 to 15 minutes or until golden. Let cool.

Combine caramels and evaporated milk in a saucepan over medium heat. Stir frequently until melted. Remove from heat; stir in liqueur or coffee. Spoon caramel filling into baked shells; let cool.

Pipe frosting onto caramel filling. Makes about 2 dozen.

Frosting:
1/2 c. shortening
1/3 c. sugar
1/3 c. evaporated milk, chilled
1/2 t. coffee liqueur or brewed coffee

Blend shortening and sugar together until fluffy; add evaporated milk and liqueur or coffee. Beat with an electric mixer on medium-high until fluffy or about 7 to 10 minutes.

Staci Meyers
Ideal, GA

Caramel-Coffee Tassies

Sausage & 3-Pepper Penne

Add a salad and garlic bread for a meal that any family would enjoy.

19.76-oz. pkg. hot Italian pork sausage, sliced into 1-inch pieces
1 green pepper, diced
1 red pepper, diced
1 yellow pepper, diced
1/2 c. onion, chopped
2 cloves garlic, minced
14-oz. can diced tomatoes
8-oz. can tomato sauce
2 t. Italian seasoning
8-oz. pkg. penne pasta, cooked
1/4 c. grated Parmesan cheese

Cook sausage in a skillet over medium-high heat until browned. Remove sausage from skillet and set aside. In same skillet, cook peppers, onion and garlic in sausage drippings until peppers are crisp-tender. Stir in tomatoes, sauce, seasoning and cooked sausage. Simmer for another one to 2 minutes or until heated through. Pour sauce over cooked pasta; mix thoroughly. Top with Parmesan cheese. Makes 6 servings.

Lorrie Haskell
Lyndeborough, NH

Delicious Dishes from your pantry

Need a last-minute dish for company or a potluck? Check your pantry to see if you have the ingredients for one of these easy recipes. For example, if you have an egg, cashews, sugar and spices, you can make Spiced Christmas Cashews. With canned corn and green beans, you can prepare Festive Corn Bake. Ravioli Taco Bake is a crowd-pleaser you'll want to serve all year! Chances are, you can make these snacks, sweets, side dishes and entrées without a trip to the store.

Grandma Mary's Shortbread

I received this wonderful recipe 20 years ago from a dear friend who was like a grandmother to me.

1 c. butter, softened
2 c. all-purpose flour
$\frac{1}{2}$ c. superfine sugar
2 T. cornstarch

Combine all ingredients in a medium bowl and knead to form a smooth dough. Roll out on a floured surface to $\frac{1}{4}$-inch thick. Cut out with a cookie or biscuit cutter. Transfer to ungreased baking sheets. Bake at 275 degrees for 45 minutes; cool. Frost with cream cheese frosting. Refrigerate until set or ready to serve. Makes about 3 dozen.

Cream Cheese Frosting:
4 oz. cream cheese, softened
$\frac{1}{4}$ c. butter, softened
1 t. vanilla extract
$2\frac{1}{4}$ c. powdered sugar

With an electric mixer on medium speed, beat cream cheese and butter together. Add vanilla and mix well. On low speed, add powdered sugar until mixed. Beat on high speed for one minute.

Kerry McNeil
Anacortes, WA

Grandma Mary's Shortbread

Chicken-Corn Tortilla Soup

Chicken-Corn Tortilla Soup
Yummy soup that's ready in a flash!

3 12¹/₂-oz. cans white chicken meat,
    undrained
4 c. fat-free, less-sodium chicken broth
1 c. salsa
1 c. corn tortilla chips, crushed
¹/₂ c. fresh cilantro, chopped
2 t. lime juice
¹/₄ t. pepper
Garnish: shredded Cheddar cheese, sour
    cream

Shred chicken, using 2 forks, in a large saucepan. Add broth and salsa; bring to a boil over medium-high heat. Add tortilla chips; reduce heat and simmer for 10 minutes. Stir in cilantro, lime juice and pepper. Serve immediately. Garnish, if desired. Serves 8.

Spiced Christmas Cashews are great for quick snacks. Ordinary ingredients make Chicken-Corn Tortilla Soup and Mandy's Easy Cheesy Chicken Casserole delicious!

Festive Corn Bake
A crispy, buttery topping sets this corn casserole apart from the rest!

15¹/₄-oz. can corn, drained
14¹/₂-oz. can French-style green beans, drained
10³/₄-oz. can cream of celery soup
8-oz. container sour cream
1 onion, chopped
1 sleeve round buttery crackers, crushed
1 c. sliced almonds
¹/₂ c. butter, melted

Mix together corn and green beans; spread in an ungreased 2-quart casserole dish. Stir together soup, sour cream and onion; spread over vegetables. Mix crackers, almonds and butter together; spread over soup layer. Bake at 350 degrees for 30 minutes or until bubbly. Serves 6.

Nancy Schroeder
McPherson, KS

Spiced Christmas Cashews

Mandy's Easy Cheesy
Chicken Casserole

Mandy's Easy Cheesy Chicken Casserole

This is a recipe that I created by combining a few different recipes. My husband loves it and it is always a hit at reunions and potlucks.

3 to 4 cooked chicken breasts, chopped
16-oz. pkg. wide egg noodles, cooked
24-oz. container sour cream
2 10³/₄-oz. cans cream of chicken soup
8-oz. pkg. shredded Cheddar cheese
8-oz. pkg. shredded mozzarella cheese
1 sleeve round buttery crackers, crushed
¹/₄ c. margarine, melted
2 T. poppy seed

Combine chicken, noodles, sour cream, soup and cheeses in a large bowl. Pour into a lightly greased 13"x9" baking dish. Mix together cracker crumbs and margarine; sprinkle over top. Sprinkle poppy seed over cracker crumbs. Bake at 350 degrees for 25 to 30 minutes or until crackers are crispy and golden and cheese is melted. Serves 8 to 10.

Mandy Wheeler
Ashland, KY

Spiced Christmas Cashews

These well-seasoned cashews are sweet, salty and crunchy...and oh-so snackable! Everybody raves about them. I often make 10 to 12 batches for gifts during the holiday season...maybe even more!

1 egg white
1 T. water
2 9³/₄-oz. cans salted cashews
¹/₃ c. sugar
1 T. chili powder
2 t. salt
2 t. ground cumin
¹/₂ t. cayenne pepper

Whisk together egg white and water in a large bowl. Add cashews; toss to coat. Transfer to a colander; drain for 2 minutes. In a separate bowl, combine sugar and spices; add cashews and toss to coat. Arrange in a single layer on a greased 15"x10" jelly-roll pan. Bake, uncovered, at 250 degrees for 1¹/₄ hours, stirring once. Cool on a wire rack. Store in an airtight container. Makes about 3¹/₂ cups.

Paula Marchesi
Lenhartsville, PA

Ravioli Taco Bake

I was looking for something easy and different to take to our church potluck suppers so I came up with this recipe. Not only was it a hit...I came home with an empty dish and over 50 people wanting the recipe!

1¹/₂ lbs. ground beef
³/₄ c. water
1¹/₄-oz. pkg. taco seasoning mix
40-oz. can meat-filled ravioli
8-oz. pkg. shredded Cheddar cheese
Garnish: sliced black olives

Brown ground beef in a large skillet over medium heat; drain. Stir in water and seasoning mix. Reduce heat; simmer for 8 to 10 minutes. Place ravioli in a lightly greased 13"x9" baking pan; spoon beef mixture over top. Sprinkle with cheese. Bake, uncovered, at 350 degrees for 25 to 30 minutes or until cheese is melted and bubbly. If desired, sprinkle with olives before serving. Serves 6 to 8.

Margie Kirkman
High Point, NC

111

Loopy Ornaments
(also shown on page 8)
- pinking shears
- felt (we used 8 colors, including white)
- plastic basin
- liquid dishwashing detergent (without scents or dyes)
- green and red wool roving
- rubber gloves (optional)
- craft knife and cutting mat
- fabric glue
- yarn

1. For each ornament, use pinking shears to cut one 2¹/₂" and two 1¹/₂" diameter white felt circles. Cut seven ¹/₂"x5" different-colored felt strips.
2. Follow *Felted Wool Balls* (page 140) to make an all-wool ball with roving. Cut the ball in half with the craft knife; set aside one half for another ornament.
3. Fold the strips into loops and glue to the front and back of the large white circle. Loop and glue a 12" yarn length to the back for the hanger.
4. Center and glue a small circle on the front and back of the ornament. Glue the wool half-ball to the ornament front.

Snowflower Ornaments
(also shown on page 8)
- self-covered button (we used 1¹/₈" to 1¹/₂" dia. buttons)
- dotted fabric scrap
- white felt
- fabric glue
- ribbon

For each ornament, cover a button with a fabric scrap. Cut 3 white felt circles (ours are 1", 2" and 3" diameter). Cut slits around the medium and large circles, ¹/₂" and ³/₄" deep. Glue the covered button and medium circle to the large circle. Fold and glue an 8" ribbon length to the back for the hanger. Glue the small circle on the back to finish the ornament.

Felt Tree Topper
(also shown on page 8)
- water-soluble fabric marker
- ivory, red, green, rust, light blue and blue wool felt scraps
- pinking shears
- ecru embroidery floss
- polyester fiberfill
- hot glue gun
- 1¹/₂" dia. self-covered button
- dotted fabric scrap

1. Enlarge the patterns on page 145 to 145%; cut out. Draw around the patterns with the marker and cut from felt: 8 small circles from 4 different colors, one ivory circle with triangular cutouts and 4 red petals. Cut a green felt circle slightly smaller than the ivory circle. Using pinking shears, cut 2 green felt base pieces and a blue felt circle slightly larger than the ivory circle.
2. For the reverse appliqués, center and pin the ivory circle over the green circle and topstitch along the cutout edges. Zigzag ¹/₄" from the outer edge of the circle (we used contrasting thread to highlight the stitching details for added whimsy). Sew the petals in place. Use 6 strands of embroidery floss and *French Knots* (page 139) to add the small circles.

3. Leaving the top and bottom open, sew the base pieces together along the long edges. Center and pin the ivory circle on the blue circle; topstitch, leaving a 2" opening at the bottom. Stuff the topper and insert the top of the base in the opening; hot glue in place, being careful not to glue the top closed.

4. Cover the button with the fabric scrap. Pulling the thread tightly to tuft the topper, sew the button to the topper front.

Dangling Ornaments
(also shown on page 11)
- pinking shears
- tracing paper
- felt (we used 8 colors)
- yarn and yarn needle
- ³/₈" dia. wood beads

For each ornament, use pinking shears and the patterns on page 144 to cut one large circle and 2 of each remaining circle size from felt. Knot one end and thread a 14" yarn length alternately through a bead and a felt circle (working from small to large and back to small circles). Tie a loop at the top for the hanger.

Felted Ball Wreath
(continued from page 12)
2. Using 6 strands of floss, run the needle through the bottom of a large ball (Fig. 1) and tie it to the 2 center wires of the wreath form. Repeat with the remaining large balls.

Fig. 1

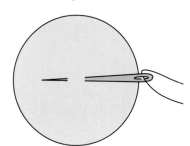

3. Attach each medium ball to the outer wire and each small ball to the inner wire. Spot glue the balls to each other for stability.

4. Add a ribbon bow and streamers to the outer wire at the top of the wreath form. Attach a ring to the back for the hanger.

Sweet Gift Card Holder
(continued from page 16)
1. Using the patterns on page 144, cut a bird and leaves from felt and a felted wool wing.

2. For the card holder, arrange and pin the appliqués on the top half of a 4¹/₂"x6" felted wool piece.

3. Using 6 strands of floss, work *Stem Stitch* (page 139) branches and attach the leaves, bird and wing with *Running Stitches*. Add a *Satin Stitch* beak and a *French Knot* eye.

4. Fold the holder and join the sides with *Running Stitches*. Sew the fastener to the inside; then, glue the ribbon around the top of the holder, knotting the ends.

5. To personalize, string the beads on floss; knot the ends. Sew the beaded strand to a corner of the gift card holder.

Needle-Felted Stockings
(continued from page 13)

2. Follow *Felted Wool Balls* (page 140) and use roving to cover the foam balls and to make 2 additional all-wool balls. Cut the all-wool balls in half. String the foam-based balls on the ends of an 18" yarn length; fold in half and tie a knot 4" from the fold for the hanger.

3. Pin layered felt and fabric circles to the stocking front; sew the pieces together in a freeform manner. Hot glue a half-ball to each center.

4. Follow *Needle Felting* (page 140) to apply stripes, a heel and a toe to the stocking front with wool roving. Sew lines across the roving.

5. Matching wrong sides, layer the stocking pieces. Using a ¹/₄" seam allowance and catching the hanger loop in the heel-side seam, sew the stocking pieces together along the side and bottom edges.

Cream Stocking
- ¹/₃ yard of cream wool felt
- red wool felt
- plastic basin
- liquid dishwashing detergent (without scents or dyes)
- red, blue and green wool roving
- two 1" dia. foam balls
- rubber gloves (optional)
- yarn needle
- red yarn
- ³/₄" dia. shank button
- needle felting tool and mat

1. Enlarge the patterns on page 145 to 200%. Use the patterns and cut 2 cream felt stocking pieces and one red felt flower.

2. Follow *Felted Wool Balls* (page 140) and use roving to cover the foam balls. String the balls on the ends of an 18" yarn length; fold in half and tie a knot 4" from the fold for the hanger.

3. Sew the flower to the stocking front. Sew the button to the center.

4. Follow *Needle Felting* (page 140) to apply a heel, a toe and other design elements to the stocking front with wool roving. Sew freeform lines on the roving.

5. Matching wrong sides, layer the stocking pieces. Using a ¹/₄" seam allowance and catching the hanger loop in the heel-side seam, sew the stocking pieces together along the side and bottom edges.

Red Stocking
- ¹/₃ yard of red wool felt
- plastic basin
- liquid dishwashing detergent (without scents or dyes)
- wool roving in assorted colors
- two 1" dia. foam balls
- rubber gloves (optional)
- yarn needle
- red yarn
- needle felting tool and mat

1. Enlarge the pattern on page 145 to 200%. Use the pattern and cut 2 felt stocking pieces.

2. Follow steps 2, 4 and 5 of the Cream Stocking to make the hanger, apply the roving design elements and assemble the stocking.

Cell Phone Cozy
(continued from page 17)

1. Cut a 7"x5³/₄" wool felt piece. Refer to Fig. 1 to mark off the stitching area.

Fig. 1

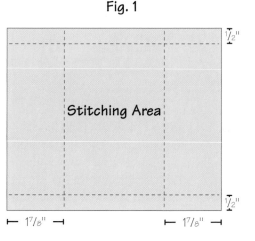

2. Enlarge the patterns on page 144 to 122%. Using the patterns, cut 2 felt leaves and one flower and flower center each from felt and fabric (we cut the centers with pinking shears). Arrange and pin the flowers and leaves in the stitching area and draw curly stems with the marker. Sew over the stem lines and hand- or machine-sew the flowers and leaves in place. Remove any marker lines with a damp cotton swab. Attach brads through the flower centers.

3. Follow *Needle Felting* (page 140) to apply berries with wool roving.

4. Use freeform stitching lines to sew rickrack along the top edge. Matching right sides, sew the short ends together. Finger press the seam allowances open at the center back; sew the bottom edges together. Clip the corners and turn the cozy right side out.
5. Thread the clasp on a 1"x2" felt strip; fold and sew the strip ends to the inside back of the cozy.

Woolly Pincushions
(continued from page 18)
3. Tie one end of a 12" floss length tightly around the center of fifteen 1¹/₂" floss lengths. Run the needle with the remaining floss end through the small ball, tie a knot and leaving 3", continue through the large ball and the center of the 2" felt circles; knot the end.
4. Hot glue the large ball to the top circle and the bottom circle to the inverted gelatin mold.

Red Pincushion
• plastic basin
• liquid dishwashing detergent (without scents or dyes)
• red and blue wool roving
• 3¹/₂" dia. foam ball
• rubber gloves (optional)
• tracing paper
• red wool felt
• needle felting tool
• 5 red pearlized pins
• hot glue gun
• mini sauce bowl

1. Follow *Felted Wool Balls* (page 140) to cover the foam ball with red roving. Using the pattern on page 144, cut 5 felt flowers.
2. Follow *Needle Felting* (page 140) and use blue roving to apply the flower centers and felt flowers to the ball. Insert a pin through each flower center.
3. Hot glue the pincushion to the inverted bowl.

Blue Pincushion
• plastic basin
• liquid dishwashing detergent (without scents or dyes)
• cream and light blue wool roving
• 1" dia. foam ball
• 2¹/₂" dia. foam ring
• rubber gloves (optional)
• craft knife
• embroidery scissors
• green embroidery floss
• scallop-edged scissors
• blue felt
• hot glue gun
• wood napkin ring
• needle-nose jewelry pliers
• small charm with jump ring

1. Follow *Felted Wool Balls* (page 140) to cover the foam ball and ring with wool roving. Cut a slit through the center of the ball for the embroidery scissors to fit in. Wind a floss length around and around the ring and secure the ends.
2. Scalloping the edges, cut a 3" diameter felt circle.
3. Hot glue the ball (with the slit at the top), felted ring, scalloped circle and napkin ring together. Attach the charm to the handle with pliers; then, insert the embroidery scissors in the pincushion.

Chair-back Swags
(also shown on page 21)
Welcome everyone to the table with colorful chair-back swags. Tie the end of each greenery cluster with florist's wire (we used a combination of fresh and artificial greenery, including holly with berries). Wire small vintage ornaments to the cluster and tie to the chair back with a simple ribbon bow with notched ends.

Pleated Half Apron
(also shown on page 26)
• vintage linen (our hemmed and embroidered piece is 32"w)
• 2³/₄ yards of 1¹/₂"w grosgrain ribbon
• liquid fray preventative (optional)

(continued on page 116)

1. For the apron skirt, trim the linen piece to the desired height plus 1" (we trimmed ours to 21" high). Hem the sides and bottom if necessary. Press the top edge 1/2" to the wrong side twice; topstitch.

2. To add pleats, mark the center of the topstitched edge with a pin and follow Fig. 1 to pin pleats along the top edge. Continue on each side of center for as many pleats as you like.

Fig. 1

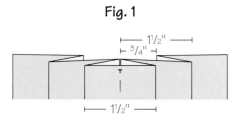

3. Press the pleats and baste along the top edge. Center and pin the ribbon tie so it overlaps the top edge of the skirt; topstitch. Trim the tie ends and apply fray preventative, if desired.

Pocketed Half Apron
(also shown on page 26)
- kraft paper
- 1/2 yard of floral pocket fabric
- 26" square of green lining fabric
- 1 1/8 yards of dotted fabric for apron front and waistband/ties
- 3/4 yard of rickrack
- 1/8 yard of red fabric for flower
- pinking shears
- heavy-duty thread

Use a 1/2" seam allowance for all sewing unless otherwise noted. This apron rests below the waist. Adjust the size of the pieces (and yardages) as needed to fit.

1. Cut a 25" diameter circle from kraft paper. Fold the circle in half and cut a pocket piece this size. Unfold the pattern and cut a circle from lining fabric. Follow Fig. 1 to trim away the top.

Fig. 1

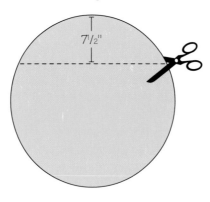

2. Using the trimmed lining piece as a pattern, cut the apron front. Cut two 7"x26" ties and a 7"x23 1/2" waistband.

3. Press the straight edge of the pocket 1/4" to the wrong side twice. Pin rickrack along the back of the pressed edge; topstitch, catching the rickrack in the stitching. Baste the pocket to the apron front along the raw edges. Topstitch from top to bottom to divide the pocket into 2 equal sections.

4. Matching right sides, pin and sew the lining to the apron front along the curved edge; clip curves, turn right side out and press.

5. Sew each end of the waistband to a tie. Press the ends and one long edge 1/2" to the wrong side. Center and sew the unpressed edge of the waistband on the apron; press the seam allowances toward the waistband. Matching wrong sides, fold the pressed edge of the waistband/tie to the back; pin, then topstitch along the bottom and side edges.

6. For the flower, stack the red and pocket fabrics right sides up. Cutting through both layers, use pinking shears to cut a 1 1/2"x32" fabric strip. Using heavy-duty thread, baste along one long edge and pull tight to create a ruffle; knot the thread ends. Coil the ruffle into a flower shape and tack the flower to the apron.

Red-Trimmed Bib Apron
(also shown on page 27)
- vintage tablecloth for skirt
- 5/8 yard of vintage-look fabric for bib and pockets
- water-soluble fabric marker
- 5 1/4 yards of extra-wide double-fold bias tape for binding
- clear nylon thread
- three 12" lengths of 3/16"w grosgrain ribbon
- 3/8 yard of fabric for waistband/ties

Match right sides and use a 1/2" seam allowance for all sewing unless otherwise noted. If you wish, cut patterns from paper first and adjust the height or width of the pieces (and yardages) as needed to fit.

1. Cut the skirt piece the desired size (we cut ours 42"wx18¹/₂"h). Cut two 10¹/₂"wx12¹/₂"h bib and two 9¹/₄"wx8¹/₂"h pocket pieces.

2. Matching wrong sides, baste the bib pieces together. To cut the "V" shape, fold the bib in half, matching long edges. Place a mark on the fold 5" from the top. Draw a line from the mark to the opposite top corner. Cut along the drawn line; unfold.

3. For each pocket "V," match short ends and fold the pocket in half. Mark the fold 2¹/₂" from the top, draw a line to the opposite top corner and cut; unfold.

4. Sandwich and pin the top edges of the bib and pockets in the fold of a bias tape length, mitering at the "V." Using nylon thread, zigzag the bias tape to each piece. Tack a grosgrain bow to the bottom of each "V."

5. Sandwich and pin each side of the bib in the fold of a bias tape length, leaving about 20" extra bias tape at the top on each side for ties; zigzag.

6. Sandwich and pin the bottom and sides of the skirt in the fold of the bias tape, mitering at the corners; zigzag in place. Press the bottom and sides of each pocket ¹/₂" to the wrong side; trim the excess. Pin and zigzag the pockets to the skirt (ours are 8¹/₂" from each side and 6¹/₂" from the bottom).

7. Beginning and ending about 7" from the corners, baste along the top edge of the skirt. Gather the basted area to fit the width of the bib; knot the thread ends. Cut two 3"x72" waistband/tie strips (each strip will need to be pieced).

8. Matching raw edges, center and pin, then sew the bib on one waistband/tie strip. Repeat to sew the skirt to the bottom of the strip. Matching right sides, pin the remaining waistband/tie strip to the first strip. Leaving the skirt and bib areas unstitched, sew along the long edges and short ends of the ties. Clip the corners, turn right side out and press, turning the raw edges of the waistband under. Pin, then topstitch around the entire waistband/tie.

Full Cinched Apron
(also shown on page 27)
- vintage tablecloth for the apron (at least 35"x48")
- water-soluble fabric marker
- 1³/₈ yards of jumbo rickrack
- ³/₄ yard of fabric for skirt backs
- ¹/₃ yard of fabric for pocket
- two ³/₄" dia. buttons

Match right sides and use a ¹/₂" seam allowance for all sewing unless otherwise noted. If you wish, cut patterns from paper first and adjust the height or width of the pieces (and yardages) as needed to fit.

1. Cut a 26"x46¹/₂" apron piece (we cut ours from the center design of the tablecloth). To shape the apron, match long edges and fold the piece in half. Follow Fig. 1 to mark a point 8" from the fold on the top short end. Mark the cutting line and trim the fabric.

Fig. 1

2. Enlarge the patterns on page 147 to 200%. Align the blue line on the neckline opening pattern with the fold at the narrow end of the apron. Cut away the opening. Press the neckline ¹/₂" to the wrong side, clipping as needed. Zigzag rickrack along the neckline.

3. Cut two 11"x25" skirt backs. Press the top short end and one long edge of one piece ¹/₄" to the wrong side twice; topstitch. Press the top short end and the opposite long edge of the remaining piece ¹/₄" to the wrong side twice; topstitch.

4. Use the pocket pattern to cut 2 pockets (one in reverse). Press the top of each pocket ¹/₂" to the wrong side. Zigzag rickrack along the top edge. Press the curved side and bottom edge of each pocket ¹/₂" to the wrong side, clipping the curves.

(continued on page 118)

5. With right sides up and matching raw side edges, pin a pocket to each skirt back 1½" below the top edge; baste. Topstitch along the curved side and bottom edge of each pocket.

6. Matching bottom edges, sew a skirt back to the apron along each apron side. Press the seam allowances open. Press the remaining long raw edges of the apron front (bib) ¼" to the wrong side twice; topstitch.

7. Press the bottom edge of the entire apron ½", then 1½" to the wrong side; hem.

8. Cut two 4½"x18" tablecloth pieces for the back cross straps. Turn the long edges ¼" to the wrong side twice; topstitch. Sew one end of each strap to the top of the apron front. Cross the straps and pin the ends to the loose corners of the apron skirt back. Try the apron on and adjust the straps as needed.

9. Cinch and pin each side at the waistline to fit. Secure the cinched areas with buttons. Topstitch the straps in place.

Green-Trimmed Bib Apron
(also shown on page 27)
• ⅝ yard of print fabric for bib and skirt
• ¾ yard of solid fabric

Match right sides and use a ½" seam allowance for all sewing unless otherwise noted. If you wish, cut patterns from paper first and adjust the height or width of the pieces (and yardages) as needed to fit.

1. Cut a 13"wx12½"h bib and a 21½"wx15½"h skirt piece. From solid fabric, cut one 3"x22" and one 3"x40" neck strap, one 80"x5" ruffle (this will need to be pieced), one 13"x3" waistband and two 41"x3" waistband ties.

2. Press the short ends of the skirt ¼" to the wrong side twice; topstitch. Press both short ends and one long edge of the ruffle ¼" to the wrong side twice; hem. Baste along the top edge of the ruffle. Gather the ruffle to fit the long bottom edge of the skirt. Pin, then sew the ruffle to the skirt. Press the seam allowances toward the skirt and topstitch.

3. Press the short ends and one long edge of the waistband ½" to the wrong side. Baste along the top edge of the skirt for about 5" on each side. Gather to fit the waistband and knot the thread ends. Pin, then sew the unpressed edge of the waistband to the skirt; press the seam allowances toward the waistband. Fold and pin the remaining long edge of the waistband to the back; topstitch, leaving the short ends unstitched.

4. Press one short end and both long edges of each waistband tie ¼" to the wrong side twice; topstitch. Pleating as necessary, tuck the raw end of one tie in each end of the waistband; topstitch.

5. Press one short end and both long edges of each neck strap ¼" to the wrong side twice; topstitch.

6. Press the short ends and the bottom long edge of the bib ¼" to the wrong side twice; topstitch. Press the top edge of the bib ¼" to the wrong side twice. Tuck and pin the raw end of one strap under the fold at each corner of the bib, pleating the strap; topstitch the top of the bib. Overlapping edges by ½", center and pin the waistband over the bottom of the bib; topstitch.

Natural Wreath
(also shown on page 29)

Use florist's wire to attach artificial cedar picks to a wood or wire wreath form (we used a stained 12" diameter inner circle from an embroidery hoop). Hot glue circles and scraps cut from birch bark sheets and then pinecone halves to the wreath. Tuck in live cedar sprigs to add that fresh cedar scent to your light & airy wreath.

Hanging Log Feeder
(also shown on page 32)
- handsaw
- fallen or purchased log (we used a 2" dia. birch log)
- drill with bits
- dowel (optional)
- Bird Food Mix (recipe on page 31)
- $^{3}/_{16}$"x2" eye screw
- leather lace

1. Cut a log the length you want. For perches, trim the branches to 2" or 3" from the log, or drill small holes and add dowel lengths. Drill a 1" diameter hole above each perch for the Bird Food Mix. Drill a hole in the top of the log and add the eye screw.

2. For the hanger, knot the ends of the leather lace together and attach to the eye screw with a lark's head knot (Fig. 1).

Fig. 1

3. Add Bird Food Mix to the holes, hang the feeder and let the banquet begin!

Paper Snowflakes
(continued from page 34)

1. Cut an 8"x8" parchment square for each snowflake. Punch 1" snowflakes from the excess paper to scatter on your tree.

2. Fold each square in half. Follow Fig. 1 to lightly mark the top edge and center on each piece where shown.

Fig. 1

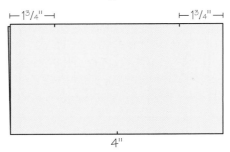

3. Carefully aligning the marks, follow Figs. 2-4 to fold each piece into thirds and then in half, forming a cone shape.

Fig. 2

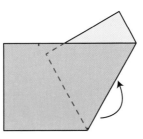

Fig. 3

Fig. 4

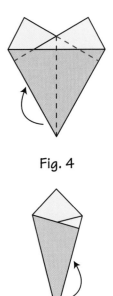

4. Enlarge the patterns on page 151 to 160%. Aligning the dashed lines on each pattern with the folded edges of a cone, transfer the solid pattern lines to the paper cone. Carefully cut through all thicknesses along the transferred lines. Unfold the snowflake.

5. For the hanger, tie nylon thread through a hole pierced in the snowflake. Sprinkle the tree with the hanging and punched paper snowflakes.

Log Tote
(also shown on page 36)
- 17½"x35½" piece of heavyweight fusible interfacing
- 18½"x36½" piece of heavyweight fabric for lining
- 18½"x36½" piece of heavyweight fabric for tote front
- 3 yards of jumbo rickrack
- 3 yards of 1"w cotton strapping
- embroidery floss
- 4 decorative brads

1. Center and fuse the interfacing on the wrong side of the lining fabric. Matching right sides and leaving an opening for turning, use a ½" seam allowance to sew the lining and tote front together. Clip the corners, turn right side out and press. Sew the opening closed. Topstitch around the edges.

2. Center and zigzag the rickrack on the strapping. Beginning where shown (Fig. 1), pin the strapping to the tote front, allowing for a 15" handle loop at each end. Overlapping the strapping ends, fold the top end under ½" (trimming as needed) and pin in place. Zigzag the strapping to the tote along each long edge of the strapping.

Fig. 1

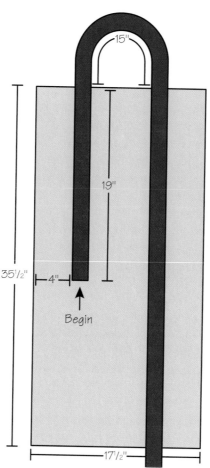

3. Using 6 strands of floss and long *Straight Stitches* (page 139), work four 3" stars on one end of the tote (for a rustic look, we tied the beginning and ending knots on the tote front). Attach a brad at the center of each star and bring in the logs for the fire!

Woodland Throw
(also shown on page 37)
Read Crochet on pages 142-143 before beginning.

 ■■□□ **EASY +**

Finished Size: 57½" x 69" (146 cm x 175.5 cm)

Materials
Medium Weight Yarn 〔MEDIUM 4〕
  [3.5 ounces, 208 yards (100 grams, 190 meters) per skein]: 18 skeins
Crochet hook, size G (4 mm) **or** size needed for gauge
Yarn needle

Gauge: In pattern,
  14 sts and 11 rows = 4" (10 cm)
  Each Strip = 9½" (24.25 cm) wide

Gauge Swatch: 7"w x 4"h (17.75 cm x 10 cm)
  Work same as Strip through Row 11.

Stitch Guide

Front Post Double Crochet
(abbreviated FPdc)
YO, insert hook from **front** to **back** around post of st indicated, YO and pull up a loop even with loops on hook (Fig. 3, page 143), (YO and draw through 2 loops on hook) twice. Skip sc behind FPdc.

Beginning 3-dc Cluster
Ch 2, ★ YO, insert hook in st indicated, YO and pull up a loop even with loops on hook, YO and draw through 2 loops on hook; repeat from ★ once **more**, YO and draw through all 3 loops on hook.

3-dc Cluster
★ YO, insert hook in sc indicated, YO and pull up a loop even with loops on hook, YO and draw through 2 loops on hook; repeat from ★ 2 times **more**, YO and draw through all 4 loops on hook.

Front Post Cluster
(abbreviated FP Cluster)
★ YO, insert hook from **front** to **back** around post of dc indicated (Fig. 3, page 143), YO and pull up a loop even with loops on hook, YO and draw through 2 loops on hook; repeat from ★ 2 times **more**, YO and draw through all 4 loops on hook.

Decrease
Pull up a loop in next 2 sts, YO and draw through all 3 loops on hook **(counts as one sc)**.

Strip (Make 6)
Ch 26 **loosely**.

Row 1 (Right side): Dc in fourth ch from hook **(3 skipped chs count as first dc)** and in each ch across: 24 dc.

Note: Loop a short piece of yarn around any stitch to mark Row 1 as **right** side and bottom edge.

Row 2: Ch 1, turn; sc in each dc across.

Row 3: Ch 3 **(counts as first dc, now and throughout)**, turn; dc in next 6 sc, work FPdc around dc one row **below** next sc, dc in next 2 sc on previous row, work FP Cluster around dc one row **below** next sc, skip sc behind FP Cluster, dc in next 2 sc, work FP Cluster around next dc from last FP Cluster made, skip sc behind FP Cluster, dc in next 2 sc, work FPdc around dc one row **below** next sc, dc in last 7 sc.

Row 4: Ch 1, turn; sc in each st across.

Row 5: Ch 3, turn; dc in next 6 sc, work FPdc around next FPdc, dc in next 2 sc, skip next sc, work FP Cluster around dc one row **below** next sc, skip sc behind FP Cluster, dc in next 2 sc, work FP Cluster around next dc from last FP Cluster made, skip sc behind FP Cluster, dc in next 2 sc, work FPdc around next FPdc, dc in last 7 sc.

Repeat Rows 4 and 5 until Strip measures approximately 66" (167.5 cm) from beginning ch, ending by working Row 5; do **not** finish off.

Border
Rnd 1: Ch 1, do **not** turn; work 195 sc evenly spaced across end of rows; working in free loops of beginning ch (Fig. 2, page 143), 3 sc in first ch, decrease, sc in next 20 chs, 3 sc in next ch; work 195 sc evenly spaced across end of rows; working across last row, 3 sc in first dc, decrease, sc in each st across to last dc, 3 sc in last dc; join with slip st to first sc: 444 sc.

Rnd 2: Work Beginning 3-dc Cluster in same st, ch 1, skip next sc, ★ (work 3-dc Cluster in next sc, ch 1, skip next sc) across to center sc of next corner 3-sc group, (work 3-dc Cluster, ch 1) 3 times in center sc, skip next sc; repeat from ★ around; join with slip st to top of Beginning 3-dc Cluster: 230 3-dc Clusters and 230 ch-1 sps.

Rnd 3: Ch 1, sc in same st and in each ch-1 sp and each 3-dc Cluster around working 3 sc in center 3-dc Cluster of each corner 3-dc Cluster group; join with slip st to first sc, finish off: 468 sc.

Assembly
Place two Strips with **wrong** sides together and bottom edges at the same end. Working through both loops, whipstitch Strips together (Fig. 5, page 143), beginning in center sc of first corner 3-sc group and ending in center sc of next corner 3-sc group.
Repeat for remaining Strips.

Edging
With **right** side facing, join yarn with sc in any sc (see *Joining With Sc*, page 143); sc evenly around entire Afghan working 3 sc in center sc of each corner 3-sc group; join with slip st to first sc, finish off.

Knit Tree Skirt
(also shown on page 39)
Read Knit on pages 141-142 before beginning.

 **EASY**

Finished Size: 17¹/₂" (44.5 cm) length; approx 44" (112 cm) from point to point

Materials
Medium Weight Yarn [3.5 ounces, 208 yards (100 grams, 190 meters) per skein]: 5 skeins
31" (78.5 cm) Circular needle, size 7 (4.5 mm) **or** size needed for gauge
Markers

Gauge: In Stockinette Stitch, 20 sts = 4" (10 cm)

Note: Do **not** join. Skirt is worked back and forth on circular needle.

Bottom Border
Cast on 570 sts.

Rows 1-4: Knit across.

Row 5: K3 (Side Border), ★ place marker (see Markers, page 141), K 94; repeat from ★ across to last 3 sts (Side Border), K3.

Body
Row 1 (Decrease row): K3, ★ [slip 1 as if to **knit**, K1, PSSO (Figs. 5a & b, page 142)], knit across to within 2 sts of next marker, K2 tog (Fig. 3, page 141); repeat from ★ across to last 3 sts, K3: 558 sts.

Row 2 (Wrong side): K3, purl across to last 3 sts, K3.

Rows 3-10: Repeat Rows 1 and 2, 4 times: 510 sts.

Row 11: Knit across.

Row 12: K3, purl across to last 3 sts, K3.

Rows 13 and 14: Repeat Rows 11 and 12.

Rows 15-112: Repeat Rows 1-14, 7 times: 90 sts.

Top Border
Rows 1-5: Knit across.

Bind off all sts in **knit**.

Make five 1¹/₂" (4 cm) diameter Pom-Poms (page 140) and sew a pom-pom to each point on the tree skirt.

Knit Hat Ornament
(also shown on page 40)
Read Knit on pages 141-142 before beginning.

EASY

Circumference: 8³/₄" (22 cm)

Materials
Super Fine Weight Yarn [1.76 ounces, 213 yards (50 grams, 195 meters) per skein]: 1 skein
Straight knitting needles, size 2 (2.75 mm) **or** size needed for gauge
Tapestry needle
Embroidery floss (for the hanger)

Gauge: In Stockinette Stitch, 36 sts and 48 rows = 4" (10 cm)

Cuff
Cast on 80 sts.

Rows 1-9: (K1, P1) across.

Body
Rows 1-24: Beginning with a **knit** row, work in Stockinette Stitch.

Shaping

Row 1: K3, K2 tog (Fig. 3, page 141), K 10, [slip 1 as if to **knit**, K1, PSSO (Figs. 5a & b, page 142)], ★ K6, K2 tog, K 10, slip 1 as if to **knit**, K1, PSSO; repeat from ★ 2 times **more**, K3: 72 sts.

Row 2: Purl across.

Row 3: K2, K2 tog, K1, slip 1 as if to **knit**, K1, PSSO, ★ K4, K2 tog, K1, slip 1 as if to **knit**, K1, PSSO; repeat from ★ across to last 2 sts, K2: 56 sts.

Row 4: Purl across.

Row 5: K1, K2 tog, K1, slip 1 as if to **knit**, K1, PSSO, ★ K2, K2 tog, K1, slip 1 as if to **knit**, K1, PSSO; repeat from ★ across to last st, K1: 40 sts.

Row 6: Purl across.

Row 7: ★ K2 tog, K1, slip 1 as if to **knit**, K1, PSSO; repeat from ★ across: 24 sts.

Row 8: P2 tog across (Fig. 4, page 142): 12 sts.

Cut yarn leaving a long end for sewing. Thread needle with long end and weave needle through remaining 12 sts; gather **tightly** to close and secure end; then weave back seam (Fig. 7, page 142).

Add a 1" (2.5 cm) diameter Pom-Pom (page 140) to top of Hat if desired. Sew a floss loop to the top for the hanger.

Knit Mitten

(also shown on pages 40 and 43)
Read Knit on pages 141-142 before beginning.

 EASY

Hand Circumferences:
Child Size: 6" (15 cm)
Ornament: 2³/₄" (7 cm)

Materials
For Child Size
Medium Weight Yarn 【MEDIUM 4】
 [3.5 ounces, 223 yards (100 grams, 205 meters) per skein]: 1 skein
Straight knitting needles, size 9 (5.5 mm) **or** size needed for gauge
Stitch holders - 2
Yarn needle
Markers

For Ornament
Super Fine Weight Yarn 【SUPER FINE 1】
 [1.76 ounces, 213 yards (50 grams, 195 meters) per skein]: 1 skein
Straight knitting needles, size 2 (2.75 mm) **or** size needed for gauge
Crochet hook, C (2.75 mm) for Chain
Stitch holders - 2
Tapestry needle
Tracing paper
Heavy cardstock
Markers

Gauge: Child Size
With larger size needles and 2 strands of yarn held together, in Stockinette Stitch 16 sts and 20 rows = 4" (10 cm)
Ornament
With smaller size needles, in Stockinette Stitch 36 sts and 48 rows = 4" (10 cm)

Note: The same instructions are used for both mittens, changing yarn weight and needle size. The Child Size is worked holding 2 strands of yarn together throughout with larger size needles and the Ornament is worked with one strand of yarn with smaller size needles.

Cuff
Cast on 20 sts.

Rows 1-7: (K1, P1) across.

Body
Row 1 (Right side): Knit across increasing 6 sts evenly spaced (Figs. 1a & b, page 141): 26 sts.

Row 2: Purl across.

Thumb Gusset
Row 1: K 12, place marker (see Markers, page 141), increase in each of next 2 sts, place marker, K 12: 28 sts.

Row 2: Purl across.

Row 3: Knit across to next marker, slip marker, increase in next st, K2, increase in next st, slip marker, knit across: 30 sts.

Row 4: Purl across.

(continued on page 124)

Row 5: Knit across to next marker, slip marker, increase in next st, K4, increase in next st, slip marker, knit across: 32 sts.

Row 6: Purl across.

Note: You are now going to divide your work and make the thumb, placing sts for front and back of mitten onto st holders to be worked later.

Row 7: Knit across to next marker, remove marker, slip sts just worked onto st holder, K8, remove marker, slip remaining sts onto second st holder: 8 sts.

Thumb
Rows 1-7: Beginning with a **purl** row, work in Stockinette Stitch.

Row 8: K2 tog across (Fig. 3, page 141): 4 sts.

Cut yarn leaving a long end for sewing.

Thread needle with end and weave needle through remaining 4 sts; gather **tightly** to close and secure end.

Hand
Slip sts from second st holder onto empty needle and knit across, **turn work**; purl across; slip sts from first st holder onto empty needle and purl across: 24 sts.

Rows 1-13: Beginning with a **knit** row, work in Stockinette Stitch.

Shaping
Row 1: (K2, K2 tog) across: 18 sts.

Row 2: Purl across.

Row 3: (K1, K2 tog) across: 12 sts.

Row 4: Purl across.

Row 5: K2 tog across: 6 sts.

Cut yarn leaving a long end for sewing.

Thread needle with end and weave needle through remaining 6 sts; gather **tightly** to close and secure end.

Turn Mitten inside out and sew seam.

For each Ornament only, make 2 Mittens. Join yarn with slip st to the inside side seam of one Mitten, chain a 9½" (24 cm) length; slip st to inside side seam of second Mitten; finish off. For each tassel, cut eleven 2½" (6.5 cm) yarn lengths, bundle and fold in half. Wrap a 6" (15 cm) piece of yarn tightly around the bundle near the fold; tie a knot and sew a tassel to the top of each mitten. Enlarge the pattern on page 150 to 200%. Using the pattern, cut a mitten insert from cardstock; place the insert in the mitten.

Knit Scarf
(also shown on pages 40 and 43)
Read Knit on pages 141-142 before beginning.

 EASY

Finished Sizes:
Child Size: 6¾" x 58"
(17 cm x 147.5 cm)
Garland: 3¼" x 29"
(8.5 cm x 73.5 cm)

Materials
For Child Size
Medium Weight Yarn
   [3.5 ounces, 223 yards
   (100 grams, 205 meters) per
   skein]: 1 skein
Straight knitting needles, size 8
   (5 mm) **or** size needed
   for gauge

For Garland
Super Fine Weight Yarn
   [1.76 ounces, 213 yards
   (50 grams, 195 meters) per
   skein]: 2 skeins
Straight knitting needles, size 2
   (2.75 mm) **or** size needed
   for gauge

Gauge: Child Size

With larger size needles, in Stockinette Stitch
18 sts and 24 rows =
4" (10 cm)

Garland

With smaller size needles, in Stockinette Stitch
36 sts and 48 rows =
4" (10 cm)

Note: The same instructions are used for both sizes, changing yarn weight and needle size.

Bottom Band

Cast on 30 sts.

Rows 1-8: Knit across.

Body

Row 1 (Wrong side): K5, purl across to last 5 sts, K5.

Row 2: Knit across.

Row 3: K5, purl across to last 5 sts, K5.

Rows 4-337: Repeat Rows 2 and 3, 167 times.

Top Band

Rows 1-7: Knit across.

Bind off all sts in **knit**.

Knit Skate Ornament
(also shown on page 40)
Read Knit on pages 141-142 before beginning.

⬤⬤⬤◻ **INTERMEDIATE**

Finished Size: 4" (10 cm) from Toe to Heel

Materials

Super Fine Weight Yarn
[1.76 ounces, 213 yards
(50 grams, 195 meters)
per skein]: 1 skein
Straight knitting needles, size 2
2.75 mm) **or** size needed
for gauge
Stitch holders - 3
Tapestry needle
Tracing paper
Heavy cardstock
Lead-free stained glass solder for skate blade
Cotton twine for laces
Embroidery floss (for hanger)

Gauge: In Stockinette Stitch,
36 sts and 48 rows =
4" (10 cm)

Cuff

Cast on 44 sts.

Rows 1-7: Beginning with a **purl** row, work in Stockinette Stitch.

Body

Row 1 (Right side): K 12, K2 tog (Fig. 3, page 141), YO (Fig 2a, page 141), P1, K1, P1, YO (Fig. 2b, page 141), K2 tog, K6, K2 tog, YO, P1, K1, P1, YO, K2 tog, K 12.

Row 2: P 14, K1, P1, K1, P 10, K1, P1, K1, purl across.

Row 3: K 14, P1, K1, P1, K 10, P1, K1, P1, knit across.

Rows 4-10: Repeat Rows 2 and 3, 3 times; then repeat Row 2 once **more**.

Row 11: K 12, K2 tog, YO, P1, K1, P1, YO, K2 tog, K6, K2 tog, YO, P1, K1, P1, YO, K2 tog, K 12.

Rows 12-26: Repeat Rows 2-11 once, then repeat Rows 2-6 once **more**.

Cut yarn.

Left Heel

Note: When instructed to slip a stitch, always slip as if to **purl**, unless otherwise instructed.

Row 1: Slip 12 sts onto st holder (Right Heel), slip next 20 sts onto second st holder (Top of Foot), knit across: 12 sts.

Row 2: Purl across.

Row 3: Slip 1, knit across.

Rows 4-11: Repeat Rows 2 and 3, 4 times.

(continued on page 126)

Heel Turning: P1, P2 tog (Fig. 4, page 142), P1, **turn**; slip 1, K2, **turn**; P2, P2 tog, P1, **turn**; slip 1, K3, **turn**; P3, P2 tog, P1, **turn**; slip 1, K4, **turn**; P4, P2 tog, P1, **turn**; slip 1, K5, **turn**; P5, P2 tog, P1: 7 sts.

Slip remaining sts onto st holder; cut yarn.

Right Heel
With **right** side facing, slip 12 sts from Right Heel st holder onto empty needle.

Row 1: Knit across.

Row 2: Slip 1, purl across.

Row 3: Knit across.

Rows 4-10: Repeat Rows 2 and 3, 3 times; then repeat Row 2 once **more**.

Heel Turning: K1, K2 tog, K1, **turn**; slip 1, P2, **turn**; K2, K2 tog, K1, **turn**; slip 1, P3, **turn**; K3, K2 tog, K1, **turn**; slip 1, P4, **turn**; K4, K2 tog, K1, **turn**; slip 1, P5, **turn**; K5, K2 tog, K1; do **not** cut yarn: 7 sts.

Gusset and Instep
Row 1: With **right** side facing, pick up 5 sts along side of Right Heel (Fig. 6, page 142), slip 20 sts from Top of Foot st holder onto an empty needle, K2, P1, K1, P1, K 10, P1, K1, P1, K2, pick up 5 sts along side of Left Heel, knit 7 sts from Left Heel st holder: 44 sts.

Row 2: P 14, K1, P1, K1, P 10, K1, P1, K1, purl across.

Row 3: K 10, K2 tog, K2, P1, K1, P1, K 10, P1, K1, P1, slip 1 as if to **knit**, K1, PSSO (Figs. 5a & b, page 142), K 12: 42 sts.

Row 4: P 13, K1, P1, K1, P 10, K1, P1, K1, purl across.

Row 5: K9, K2 tog twice, YO, P1, K1, P1, YO, K2 tog, K6, K2 tog, YO, P1, K1, P1, YO, (slip 1 as if to **knit**, K1, PSSO) twice, K9: 40 sts.

Row 6: P 12, K1, P1, K1, P 10, K1, P1, K1, purl across.

Row 7: K 10, K2 tog, P1, K1, P1, K 10, P1, K1, P1, slip 1 as if to **knit**, K1, PSSO, K 10: 38 sts.

Row 8: P 11, K1, P1, K1, P 10, K1, P1, K1, purl across.

Row 9: K9, K2 tog, P1, K1, P1, K 10, P1, K1, P1, slip 1 as if to **knit**, K1, PSSO, K9: 36 sts.

Row 10: P 10, K1, P1, K1, P 10, K1, P1, K1, purl across.

Row 11: K8, K2 tog, P1, K1, P1, K 10, P1, K1, P1, slip 1 as if to **knit**, K1, PSSO, K8: 34 sts.

Row 12: P9, K1, P1, K1, P 10, K1, P1, K1, purl across.

Row 13: K5, K2 tog twice, YO, P1, K1, P1, YO, K2 tog, K6, K2 tog, YO, P1, K1, P1, YO, (slip 1 as if to **knit**, K1, PSSO) twice, K5: 32 sts.

Row 14: P8, K1, P1, K1, P 10, K1, P1, K1, purl across.

Row 15: K3, K2 tog, (K6, K2 tog) 3 times, K3: 28 sts.

Row 16: Purl across.

Row 17: K2, K2 tog, (K5, K2 tog) 3 times, K3: 24 sts.

Row 18: Purl across.

Row 19: K2, K2 tog, (K4, K2 tog) 3 times, K2: 20 sts.

Row 20: Purl across.

Row 21: K5, K2 tog, K6, K2 tog, K5: 18 sts.

Row 22: Purl across.

Cut yarn leaving a long end for weaving; thread tapestry needle with end. Weave needle through remaining sts on Row 22 and gather **tightly**. Do **not** cut yarn.

Finishing
Enlarge the skate insert pattern on page 150 to 200%. Using the pattern, cut a cardstock insert. Slip the insert into the Skate.

With **right** sides together and beginning at Toe, weave seam to first tab (Fig. 7, page 142); run yarn through sts at side until you are able to begin weaving seam again, repeat across to top of Cuff.

Roll Cuff to **right** side.

Enlarge the blade pattern on page 150 to 200%. Use the pattern to shape the skate blade from solder. Insert the blade loops through the openings in the Skate bottom; tack the loops to the back of the Skate with floss. Using twine and holes left by yarn overs, lace the Skate. Sew a floss loop to the top for the hanger.

Ice Skating Scene

(also shown on page 41)

- bell jar (ours is 11"hx12³/4" dia. at the bottom with a 15" dia. wood base)
- round mirror slightly smaller than bottom of bell jar
- heavy colored cardstock (including ivory)
- craft knife and cutting mat
- spray adhesive
- fine glitter
- mica flakes
- ivory felt
- pinking shears
- adhesive foam dots
- water-soluble fabric marker
- craft glue
- 26-gauge craft wire
- needle-nose pliers (optional)
- ¹/8" dia. hole punch
- 2 flat toothpicks
- mini vintage ornaments

For a different-size bell jar, see Sizing Patterns on page 138 to size the patterns to fit in your jar.

1. Enlarge the tree, cottage and skater patterns on page 151 to 200%. Using the patterns, cut the trees and cottage from ivory cardstock. Cut slits where shown on the patterns.

2. In a well-ventilated area, apply spray adhesive to the front and top edges of the A pieces and to the top edges only of the B pieces. Quickly sprinkle the fronts with glitter and add mica flakes along the glued edges.

3. Re-cutting slits as needed, slide each A and B pair together at the slits.

4. Cut a felt circle ¹/2" larger than the mirror, pinking the edges. Adhere the mirror to the base with foam dots. Place the felt on top and arrange the tree and cottage cutouts. Mark a curvy pond shape on the felt in front of the trees; cut out. Glue the felt, trees and cottage in place.

5. Using the enlarged patterns, cut skaters from colored cardstock and shape tiny skate blades from wire. Glue the blades to the back of the skates and add punched cardstock "pom-poms" to the skaters' hats.

6. Glue a toothpick to the back of each skater, with one end at the bottom of the skate that touches the ground. Adhere two ¹/2"-tall foam dot stacks to the mirror and glue a toothpick-backed leg to each stack. Sprinkle the scene with mica flakes. Cover with the bell jar and add ornaments around the rim of the base.

Personalized Apron

(also shown on page 45)

- 2 tea towels for apron and ruffle/pocket (ours are 18¹/4"x26¹/4")
- water-soluble fabric marker
- pinking shears
- transfer paper
- embroidery floss
- 3¹/4 yards of 1"w grosgrain ribbon
- liquid fray preventative

This sweet apron is sure to be a hit. Throw in a few baking lessons for even more fun! Match right sides and use a ¹/2" seam allowance unless otherwise noted.

1. Place the apron towel wrong side up. Follow Fig. 1 (page 128) to mark a 6"w center section on the top short end of the towel and mark each long edge 9" from the top corner. Connecting the marks, press each corner to the wrong side. Mark a line 1¹/4" from each pressed edge, extending the line to the top and side edge of the apron. To form the casings, sew along the marked lines and trim away the corners with pinking shears.

(continued on page 128)

Fig. 1

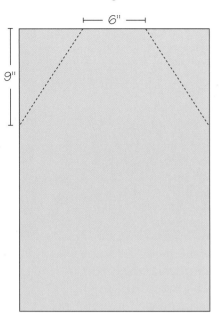

2. From the remaining towel, cut a 5"w strip from each short end and a 9¼"wx7¼"h pocket. For the ruffle, sew the strips together along one short end. Baste along the long raw edge and gather to fit the bottom edge of the apron. Pin, then sew the ruffle to the apron.
3. For the pocket, mark the bottom and side edges 2" from the corner. Connecting the marks, press each corner to the wrong side. Press the remaining edges ½" to the wrong side. Topstitch along the top edge and baste the sides and bottom.
4. Freehand or use the computer to print out a name sized to fit on the pocket. Transfer the name to the pocket. Using 6 strands of floss, work *Stem Stitch* (page 139) letters, dotting any "i's" with *French Knots*. Center and topstitch the pocket on the apron.
5. Beginning at the top, thread each ribbon end through a casing. Trim the ends and apply fray preventative.

Neck Warmer
(continued from page 47)
1. For the front of the warmer, cut each fabric piece in different-width strips at least 9" long...they shouldn't be perfect rectangles, so cut each strip a little narrower on one end, but at least 2" wide (Fig. 1).

Fig. 1

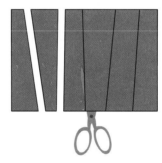

2. Matching long edges and mixing fabrics, sew strips together. Trim the edges into the desired neck warmer size, plus 1" (we trimmed ours to an 8"x18" rectangle). Press the seam allowances open.
3. Matching raw edges, baste the ends of each ribbon "handle" to the short ends of the front piece about 2" from the top and bottom.

4. Cut the flannel backing the same size as the front. Leaving an opening for turning, sew the backing to the front; trim corners and turn right side out. Fill with rice so the warmer is a little floppy and sew the opening closed. Evenly distribute the rice and pin across the warmer to divide it into sections (ours has 3 sections). Use 6 strands of floss and work *Running Stitch* (page 139) section dividers and *Blanket Stitch* around the outer edges.
5. Include instructions for use: Heat the neck warmer in a microwave on high for 2 minutes.

Hankie Blankie
(continued from page 48)
1. Cut seven 12½"x12½" muslin squares. Center a hankie on each muslin square and zigzag in place using nylon thread.
2. Arrange the hankie and fabric squares and sew the squares into 5 rows of 3 squares each. Sew the rows together.
3. Follow *Making Yo-Yo's* (page 138) and add yo-yo flowers with looped ribbon leaves to some of the squares (we cut 3½", 4½" and 5½" fabric circles for our yo-yo's). Use floss to sew folded or rolled hankies and rickrack to other squares as desired.

4. Cut a 37"x60" batting piece. Cut a 40½"x63½" backing piece; press the edges ½" to the wrong side. With the backing wrong side up, center the batting and pieced top (right side up) on the backing; pin the layers together.

5. Fold and pin the sides of the backing to the front to form the binding; topstitch. Repeat for the top and bottom binding. Using 6 strands of floss, sew through all thicknesses at the center of each block. Tie the ends together and trim.

Snowbound Tray

(continued from page 53)

1. Turn a picture frame into a captivating tray in no time. Attach drawer pulls to the sides of the frame to use as handles.

2. Glue pieced scrapbook papers to the backing to form the sky. Tear papers for snow-dusted hills and drifts.

3. Enlarge the patterns on page 152 to 182%. Use the patterns (sometimes in reverse) and cut scrapbook paper snowmen, birds and a tree. Layer and glue the shapes to the background. Draw the eyes, mouths, arms and birds' legs. Replace the backing in the tray and use ribbons to tie a layered cardstock tag to one handle.

Flap Cap

(continued from page 53)

Gauge Swatch:
4" (10 cm) diameter
Work same as Rnds 1-7 of Crown.

Stitch Guide

Beginning Decrease

(uses first 2 sc)
Pull up a loop in first 2 sc, YO and draw through all 3 loops on hook **(counts as one sc)**.

Decrease (uses next 2 sc)
Pull up a loop in next 2 sc, YO and draw through all 3 loops on hook **(counts as one sc)**.

Crown

Rnd 1 (Right side): Ch 2, 7 sc in second ch from hook; do **not** join, place marker to mark beginning of rnd (see *Markers, page 143*).

Note: Loop a short piece of yarn around any sc to mark Rnd 1 as **right** side.

Rnd 2: 2 Sc in each sc around: 14 sc.

Rnd 3: (Sc in next sc, 2 sc in next sc) around: 21 sc.

Rnd 4: (Sc in next 2 sc, 2 sc in next sc) around: 28 sc.

Rnd 5: (Sc in next 3 sc, 2 sc in next sc) around: 35 sc.

Rnd 6: (Sc in next 4 sc, 2 sc in next sc) around: 42 sc.

Rnd 7: (Sc in next 5 sc, 2 sc in next sc) around, do **not** finish off: 49 sc.

Body

Rnds 1-13: Sc in each sc around.

Left Flap

Row 1: Slip st in next sc, remove marker, ch 1, sc in same st and in next 9 sc, leaving remaining sc unworked: 10 sc.

Rows 2-8: Ch 1, turn; sc in each sc across.

Row 9: Ch 1, turn; work beginning decrease, sc in next 6 sc, decrease: 8 sc.

Row 10: Ch 1, turn; sc in each sc across.

Row 11: Ch 1, turn; work beginning decrease, sc in next 4 sc, decrease: 6 sc.

Rows 12 and 13: Ch 1, turn; sc in each sc across.

Finish off.

Right Flap

Row 1: With **right** side facing, skip 15 sc from Left Flap and join yarn with sc in next sc (see *Joining With Sc, page 143*); sc in next 9 sc, leave remaining sc unworked: 10 sc.

Rows 2-13: Work same as Left Flap; at end of Row 13, do **not** finish off: 6 sc.

(continued on page 130)

Edging

Rnd 1: Ch 1, do **not** turn; working in end of rows, skip first row, sc in next 12 rows, skip next sc, sc in next 12 sc, † skip next sc, sc in next 12 rows, skip last row, 2 sc in next sc, sc in next 2 sc, place marker in last sc made for st placement, sc in next 2 sc, 2 sc in next sc †, skip first row, sc in next 12 rows, skip next sc, sc in next 13 sc, repeat from † to † once; join with slip st to first sc: 89 sc.

Rnd 2: Ch 1, working from **left** to **right**, work reverse sc in next sc and in each sc across to first marked sc (Figs. 4a-d, page 143), † ch 25, working in back ridge of chs (Fig. 1, page 143), slip st in each ch across (Tie made), skip marked sc †, work reverse sc in next sc and in each sc across to next marked sc, repeat from † to † once, work reverse sc in next sc and in each sc around; join with slip st to first st, finish off.

Make a 1¹⁄₂" (4 cm) diameter *Pom-Pom* (page 140); attach to the top of the Crown.

Monogrammed Package
(also shown on page 55)
- transfer paper
- 12"x12" floral and solid cardstock
- bone folder or stylus
- craft glue
- floral cardstock tag
- chipboard letter for monogram
- 1"w grosgrain ribbon

Personalize your gift with a colorful monogram!

1. For a 3¹⁄₂"wx4¹⁄₂"hx1"d box, enlarge the pattern on page 154 to 121% (to make a different size box, see *Sizing Patterns* on page 138). Transfer the pattern to floral cardstock and cut along the solid lines. Score and fold the box along the dashed lines.
2. Fold, then glue the bottom tabs to the box bottom. Glue the side flaps to the pleated sides. Insert the gift; then overlap and glue the top flaps closed.
3. Glue the tag on a slightly larger solid cardstock circle. Glue the letter to the center. Wrap ribbon around the box and glue the monogram tag over the ends.

Cherry Box & Tag
(also shown on page 55)
- transfer paper
- double-sided cardstock
- craft knife and cutting mat
- green cardstock
- craft glue
- fine red and green glitter
- ribbon and fibers
- hole punch
- adhesive foam dots
- mini rickrack
- bone folder or stylus
- cellophane
- chunky red glitter
- embroidery floss
- button
- glue dot

1. For a 4"wx1¹⁄₂"hx3"d box, enlarge the box and tag patterns on page 155 to 142% (to make a different size box, see *Sizing Patterns* on page 138). Transfer the patterns to double-sided cardstock and cut along the solid lines. Cut a leaf from green cardstock; glue to the leaf on the cut out cherry. Add fine glitter to the cherry and leaf.
2. Tie ribbons and fibers through a hole punched in the tag. Use glue and a foam dot to attach the cherry and leaf to the tag. Glue rickrack along the bottom edge.

3. Score and fold the box along the dashed lines. Glue the tabs to the box sides and back. Glue the box flap to the inside.

4. For the glitter pocket, match short ends and fold, then glue the sides of a 4"x6" cellophane piece. Add chunky glitter and glue the top closed. Glue the glitter pocket inside the top of the box.

5. Glue rickrack along the top of the box. Tie floss to the button and adhere to a corner of the box with a foam dot. Place the gift in the box and close with a glue dot.

Square Gift Box
(also shown on page 56)
- square papier-mâché box (ours is 7"x7")
- ivory acrylic paint
- paintbrush
- sandpaper
- dotted scrapbook paper
- spray adhesive
- 7/8" dia. buttons
- scraps from a worn quilt
- fabric glue
- ribbons
- cardstock tag

1. Paint the box and lid; then, sand the edges for a worn look.

2. Cut paper pieces slightly smaller than the lid and sides of the box. Using spray adhesive in a well-ventilated area, adhere the pieces to the box.

3. Sew each button to layered quilt scrap circles (for fun, we cut ours with intersecting colors at the center of each circle). Glue the circles to the lid.

4. Glue layered ribbons to the sides of the lid and the tag to one side of the box.

Gift Tags
(also shown on page 59)
Family Christmas Traditions
- rub-on letters
- cardstock
- pinking shears
- "traditions" word stickers
- adhesive foam dots
- ribbon
- hole punch

For each tag, write "family" and rub the word "Christmas" on a cardstock tag with clipped corners and a pinked bottom edge (ours is 2³/₈"x4³/₄"). Add a cardstock-backed sticker to the tag with foam dots (or use small rub-on letters on a layered cardstock rectangle). Tie ribbon through the punched hole.

Holly Jolly
- solid and patterned cardstock
- ribbons
- hole punch
- "jolly" stamp
- black ink pad
- brown scrapbook chalk
- craft glue
- adhesive foam dots

To make each tag, enlarge the patterns on page 153 to 200%. Using the patterns, cut 2 cardstock leaves, 3 berries and an oval tag. Tie ribbons through the hole in the tag. Stamp "jolly" on one leaf and chalk the edges. Glue the leaves and 2 berries to the tag. Write "Christmas" on the remaining berry and adhere it to the tag with a foam dot.

December 25th
- patterned and solid cardstock
- hole punch
- craft glue
- fine glitter
- ribbons
- adhesive foam dots
- rub-on letters
- glittered wreath message stickers

For each tag, clip the corners from a 2³/₈"x4³/₄" cardstock piece. Enlarge the patterns on page 153 to 200%. Using the patterns, cut cardstock numbers and a small tag; punch a hole in both tags. Add glitter and write "to:" and "from:" on the small tag; then, tie the tags together with ribbon. Attach the numbers with foam dots and tie a ribbon around the tag. Rub-on the letters, "Dec." and apply the sticker.

Fig. 1

Garland
(also shown on page 59)
- solid and patterned double-sided cardstock
- hot glue gun
- tiny hole punch
- Christmas cards
- needle-nose jewelry pliers
- large oval chain links
- ribbon for garland
- assorted ribbons for ties

Favorite Christmas cards from years past accent this sweet & simple garland.

1. For each interlocking circle pair, enlarge the patterns on page 153 to 155%. Using the patterns, cut 2 same-size cardstock circles (one solid and one patterned). Cut slits where shown. Slide the circles together at the slits and dot loose ends with hot glue to hold in place; punch a hole near the top.
2. Cut a small circle from each Christmas card (do not cut the slit); punch a hole in the top and bottom.
3. Using pliers, join Christmas card circles to small interlocking circles with chain links. Attach to the ribbon garland.
4. Join large interlocking circles to the garland with chain links and tie ribbons around each link.

Scrapbook Caddy
(continued from page 60)
3. Use the fabric marker to freehand stems on one front felt piece, or trace the enlarged flower stems onto tissue paper and pin to the felt piece. Use 6 strands of floss and work *Running Stitch* (page 139) stems. (If using the tissue paper method, stitch through the paper; then, carefully tear the paper away.) Sew a button cluster flower at the end of each stem.
4. Use the fabric marker to place a dot in each corner of the felt rectangles, 1/4" from each edge. Sew pairs of felt rectangles together along the long edges between the dots. Sew the front and back to the sides between dots to form a rectangular tube. Pin one side of the tube to the bottom; sew the pieces together between dots. Repeat to sew the bottom to the remaining sides.
5. Arrange some scrapbook supplies on the divider (we chose scissors and markers). Pin ribbon across the divider, pinning between supplies to hold them in place. Remove the supplies, sew where pinned and trim the ends. Cut four 10" ribbon ties; set 2 aside. Sew one tie each to the center front and back of the divider (Fig. 1).

6. Draw a placement line from side to side along the inside center bottom of the caddy; hand sew the divider along the line. Sew buttons to the sides of the caddy, catching the divider side edges in the stitching.
7. Remove any visible marker lines with a damp towel. Center and sew the remaining ribbon ties to the inside front and back of the caddy. Tie the ribbons and add scrapbook supplies.

Fleece Scarf & Hat Set
(also shown on page 63)
Scarf
- 1/4 yard of striped fleece
- two 6"x7" pieces each of 3 solid fleece colors
- 1/8" dia. hole punch
- thick variegated yarn
- yarn needle

Make the scarf as long as you like...just add more fleece pieces!

Cut a 7"x36" strip of striped fleece. Matching 7" edges, stack and pin a solid piece on one end. Punch 10 to 13 holes through both layers (Fig. 1). Unpin, then place the punched edge of the solid piece under the striped piece (Fig. 2). Join the pieces with yarn *Running Stitches* (page 139) and knot the ends. Continue to connect 2 more solid pieces to this end; then, add the other 3 to the opposite end of the striped piece.

Fig. 1

Fig. 2

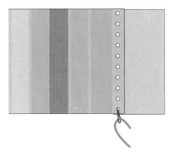

Hat

- 12"x22" piece of solid fleece for hat
- 12"x22" piece of striped fleece for lining
- embroidery floss
- thick variegated yarn

Our hat has a 22" head opening. Adjust the width of the fleece as needed. Match right sides and use a 1/2" seam allowance unless otherwise noted.

Matching short ends, fold the hat piece in half. Using 3 strands of floss, join the 11"-long sides with *Running Stitches* (page 139). Clip the corners and turn right side out. Repeat with the lining piece; do not turn right side out.

Matching seams, tuck the lining inside the hat and fold the raw edges 1/2" to the inside. Sew the bottom closed and fold up the cuff.

Tack the top corners of the hat together. Attach a 3" diameter yarn *Pom-Pom* (page 140) to the top.

Spool Family

(continued from page 64)
Make a spool person for each member of your family! Ask a grown-up for help with the glue gun. Use craft glue unless otherwise noted.

1. For each doll, cut scrapbook paper to fit around a spool; glue in place. Use the glue gun to attach a doll head to the spool. Paint a simple face. Glue floss lengths to the head for bangs.
2. Use the glue gun to attach the wheel to the bottom of Papa's spool.

3. Enlarge the patterns on page 155 to 125%. Using the patterns, cut a fleece hat to fit the doll head (large for Papa and Mama, medium for the Child and small for Baby). Using the glue gun, glue the short edges of the hat together, attach the hat to the head and add a pom-pom to the point.
4. For Papa, Mama and the Child, use the enlarged patterns and cut felt feet; glue in place. Use the glue gun to add chenille stem arms at the back of the spools.

Felt Gift Bags

(also shown on page 64)
For both Gift Bags, you'll need:
- felt
- ruler
- embroidery floss
- assorted buttons
- fabric glue

For the Blue Bag, you'll also need:
- water-soluble fabric marker
- cotton swab

Our blue bag is 5"x7" and the green pocket purse is 5"x4". Adjust the size of your bag to fit the gift you tuck inside. Read Embroidery Stitches on page 139 before you begin and use 3 strands of floss.

(continued on page 134)

Blue Bag

1. Matching short ends, fold a 5"x14" blue felt piece in half.
2. On the bag front, draw a 5" tall line for the tree trunk. Draw 4 branches (1" apart) with the shortest branch at the top and the longest at the bottom.
3. Work *Running Stitches* along the trunk and branch lines. Remove any visible markings with a damp cotton swab. Sew button "ornaments" below the branches.
4. Add a *Straight Stitch* star at the top. Sew the sides together with *Blanket Stitches* (shown) or *Running Stitches*, catching the folded ends of a 1"x10" felt strip handle in the stitching (or simply fold and glue the ends inside the bag).

Green Pocket Purse

1. Cut a 5"x10½" green felt piece and fold the short bottom end up 4" to form a pocket. Work *Running Stitches* along the sides of the pocket and flap. Fold the flap over the pocket.
2. For a cute closure, stack 2 felt circles and 2 buttons from largest to smallest and sew them together. Repeat and glue one set to the flap and the other to the pocket.
3. Work *French Knots* around each closure set.
4. Glue one end of a 6" floss length between the larger button and top felt circle on the flap. Wrap the loose end around the buttons on the pocket to close.

Hanging Birdfeeder
(also shown on page 64)
- 4" dia. clay pot with drainage hole
- 6" dia. clay saucer
- acrylic paint and paintbrush
- sandpaper
- rub-on designs
- 14" length of leather cord
- two 1" dia. painted wood beads
- Gorilla Glue®
- heavy object
- small flat chisel

Make this clever gift for your bird lover friend...just grab a grown-up for help with the glue and chisel.

1. Paint the pot and saucer. Lightly sand the edges for a worn look.
2. Add rub-ons to the pot and bottom of the saucer.
3. Fold the cord in half and knot the ends together. Thread the folded end through one bead and through the pot from the inside out. Loosely knot the folded end to keep it from slipping back into the pot (Fig. 1).

Fig. 1

4. Follow the manufacturer's instructions and run a thin bead of glue along the inner rim of the pot. Center and glue the pot on the saucer. Place a heavy object on the pot for 24 hours.
5. Scrape away any excess glue with the chisel. Untie the loose knot and thread the cord through the remaining bead. Knot the cord just above the bead.

Bag o' Birdseed
(also shown on page 64)
- birdseed in a plastic zipping bag
- paper lunch bag
- tracing paper
- ¼" dia. hole punch
- print and solid cardstock
- rub-on designs
- alphabet stamps
- black ink pad
- ribbon and rickrack trims
- craft knife and cutting mat
- adhesive foam dot
- felt scrap
- brad

Place the birdseed in the paper bag and fold the top of the bag to the back. Using the patterns on page 153, cut and punch a cardstock tag, bird and wing. Add rub-ons and stamp "Seed" on the tag; then, knot trims through the hole. Ask an adult to make the slit in the bird and insert the wing; adhere to the tag with a foam dot. For the topper, fold a felt square over the top of the bag. Punch a hole through all layers and use the brad to attach the tag to the topper.

Muffin Tin

(also shown on page 67)
- fabric glue
- small and medium rickrack
- vintage muffin tin (for decorative use only)
- double-sided holiday print cardstock
- hole punch
- Mom's Applesauce Muffins (page 67)
- ribbon
- rub-on letters
- jute twine

1. Layer and glue rickrack around the edges of the muffin tin.
2. Enlarge the patterns on page 153 to 143%. Using the patterns, cut cardstock muffin cup inserts and a tag. Place an insert and a muffin in each cup. Tie a ribbon bow through the hole in the tin. Add rub-ons to the tag and tie to the bow with twine.

Fudge Box

(also shown on page 68)
- transfer paper
- 12"x12" double-sided print cardstock
- stylus or bone folder
- craft glue
- cream cardstock
- parchment paper
- craft knife
- Graham Cracker Fudge (page 68)
- $^3/_8$"w ribbon
- alphabet stamps and ink pad
- cardstock tag
- decorative brad
- embroidery floss
- adhesive foam dots

1. Enlarge the pattern on page 157 to 133%. Transfer the pattern to the wrong side of the print cardstock; cut out. Using the stylus, score along the dashed fold lines.
2. Fold along the diagonal lines to crease; unfold. Fold the cardstock along the remaining lines and glue the flap to the opposite long edge.
3. Fold a $5^3/_4$"-long cream cardstock tray with a parchment paper liner that fits inside the box to hold the fudge.
4. When the glue on the box is completely dry, carefully push on the diagonal creases until the ends twist and meet in the center to close each end.

5. To add ribbon ties, reopen the box ends and cut a $^1/_2$" slit in the middle of each diagonal crease. Place the tray of fudge in the box. Weave a 24" ribbon through the slits at each end; close the box and tie the ribbon ends in a bow.
6. Stamp "graham cracker FUDGE" on the cardstock tag. Attach the brad, knot floss around the base and adhere the tag to the box with foam dots.

Party Mix Tin

(also shown on page 70)
- plastic zipping bag filled with Honey Popcorn & Cashews (page 70)
- tin with handle and attached scoop (ours is 7"wx6"dx9"h)
- vintage crocheted potholder with hanging loop
- snowflake print cardstock
- craft glue
- decorative chipboard label
- letter sticker
- sandpaper
- glitter
- decorative chipboard square (ours says "jolly")
- adhesive foam dots
- metal garter grip (available at fabric and scrapbook stores)
- hole punch
- twill tape

(continued on page 136)

135

1. Place the party mix in the tin. Slip the scoop handle through the hanging loop of the potholder and hook on the side of the tin.

2. Cut a cardstock tag (ours is 4³/₄"x2¹/₂"); trim the top corners. Sew around the outer edges in a freeform style. Adhere the label to the tag; add the sticker.

3. Lightly sand and glitter the edges of the chipboard square. Attach the square to the tag with a foam dot. Add dots of glitter to the tag. Slip the garter grip pin through a hole punched in the tag. Loop and sew twill tape around the garter grip hook. Attach the tag.

Rice Mix Jar

(also shown on page 73)
- pinking shears
- fabric glue
- fabric scrap
- red and white felt scraps
- 1¹/₂"w ribbon
- vintage-look jar with airtight lid (ours is 8"x4" dia.)
- tissue paper
- embroidery floss
- two ³/₄" dia. buttons
- cream cardstock
- Savory Rice Mix (page 73)

1. Pinking the edges, glue a 4"wx2³/₄"h fabric piece to a slightly larger red felt piece for the background.

2. Cut ribbon long enough to go around the jar and tie in the back. Center and glue the ribbon on the background.

3. For the pocket front, follow the *Tissue Paper Method* (page 138) to transfer the words on page 155 to a 3¹/₄"wx2"h white felt piece. Using 3 strands of floss, work *Stem Stitch* (page 139) letters, dotting the "i's" with *French Knots*. Work *Blanket Stitches* along the pocket edges; then, center and glue the sides and bottom on the background. Sew buttons on each side of the pocket.

4. Write the recipe instructions (page 73) on a 2¹/₂"wx2¹/₈"h cardstock piece and tuck in the pocket. Fill the jar with rice mix and tie the pocket tightly around the middle.

Paper Trays

(also shown on page 75)
- tracing paper
- double-sided print cardstock
- stylus or bone folder
- hole punch
- decorative brads
- snowflake punches
- flower punch
- solid cardstock
- craft glue
- mat board
- Rocky Road Bars (page 75)
- parchment paper
- 5¹/₄"x13" cellophane bags with twist ties
- rub-on letters
- oval vellum tags
- ribbons
- embroidery floss

1. For each tray, use the pattern on page 156 and cut a print cardstock piece. Score, then fold along the dashed lines.

2. Aligning the dots, punch a hole through all layers on each corner of the tray. Insert a brad through each set of holes, piercing a punched cardstock snowflake and flower in one corner. Glue more punched snowflakes to the tray.

3. Place a 4"x6" mat board piece in the base of the tray. Add bar cookies on parchment paper and place the tray in a bag; close with a twist tie.

4. For the tag, add a rub-on label to a vellum tag. Use a brad to attach punched shapes and the tag to a cardstock rectangle. Glue on more snowflakes. Thread ribbons through a hole punched in the cardstock; gather with floss and tie to the bag.

Delight-full Box
(also shown on page 76)
- purchased gift box (ours is 3"wx3"dx2"h)
- spray adhesive
- scrapbook or wrapping paper
- craft knife and cutting mat
- plastic-wrapped Lemon Delights (page 76)
- yarn
- double-sided tape
- cardstock scraps

Tell your loved one to keep these yummy cookies refrigerated until time to eat.

1. Fold the box shape; unfold. In a well-ventilated area, spray the outside of the box with adhesive. Apply paper to the box; allow to dry. Cut around the flattened box with the craft knife. Fold the covered box, tucking wrapped cookies inside.
2. Wrap yarn around the box and tie a yarn *Pom-Pom* (page 140) to the top (ours is 2" diameter).
3. Layer and tape a cardstock label on the front.

Pie Carrier
(continued from page 77)
1. Cut a mat board circle, using the bottom of the plate for a pattern. Refer to Fig. 1 to cut four 2" slits around the circle.

Fig. 1

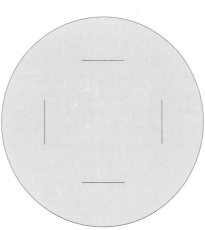

2. Paint the plate, rim and chipboard letters; allow to dry.
3. Using a thin coat of glue, apply torn paper pieces to the inside bottom of the plate. Glue the letters and add the stickers to the plate. Brush glue over the entire plate; allow to dry. Add glue to the rim and sprinkle with mica flakes.

4. For the hanger, cut two 62"-long 1¹/₂"w ribbon lengths. Cross the ribbons in the middle and thread the ends through the slits in the mat board circle. Place the circle under the plate. Pull the ribbons up around the plate. Stack the ribbons together and fold about 8" from the top. Sew the ribbons together about 4" from the fold; pull the thread tight to gather and knot the ends.
5. Tie assorted ribbons and ornaments around the gathered hanger. Insert the covered pie in the carrier.

General Instructions

Making Patterns

Place tracing or tissue paper over the pattern and draw over the lines. For a more durable pattern, use a permanent marker to draw over the pattern on stencil plastic.

Sizing Patterns

1. To change the size of the pattern, divide the desired height or width of the pattern (whichever is greater) by the actual height or width of the pattern. Multiply the result by 100 and photocopy the pattern at this percentage.

For example: You want your pattern to be 8"h, but the pattern on the page is 6"h. So 8÷6=1.33x100=133%. Copy the pattern at 133%.

2. If your copier doesn't enlarge to the size you need, enlarge the pattern to the maximum percentage on the copier. Then repeat step 1, dividing the desired size by the size of the enlarged pattern. Multiply this result by 100 and photocopy the enlarged pattern at the new percentage. (For very large projects, you'll need to enlarge the design in sections onto separate sheets of paper.) Repeat as needed to reach the desired size and tape the pattern pieces together.

Transferring Patterns to Fabric

Pick the transfer method that works best with the fabric and project you've chosen. If you choose the method using a water-soluble fabric marker, check first on a scrap piece to make sure the floss colors won't bleed when you remove the marker lines.

TISSUE PAPER METHOD

Trace the pattern onto tissue paper. Pin the tissue paper to the felt or fabric and stitch through the paper. Carefully tear the tissue paper away.

WATER-SOLUBLE FABRIC MARKER METHOD

Trace the pattern onto tissue paper or photocopy the design. Tape the pattern and fabric to a sunny window or light box; then, trace the pattern onto the fabric with the marker. After embroidering, lightly spritz the finished design with water to remove any visible markings.

Drybrushing

Use this painting technique for an aged appearance. Without dipping in water, dip an old paintbrush in paint; wipe most of the paint off onto a dry paper towel. Lightly rub the brush across the surface and repeat for desired coverage.

Making a Fabric Circle

Matching right sides, fold the fabric square in half from top to bottom and again from left to right. Tie one end of a length of string to a water-soluble fabric marker; insert a thumbtack through the string at the length indicated in the project instructions. Insert the thumbtack through the folded corner of the fabric. Holding the tack in place and keeping the string taut, mark the cutting line (Fig. 1).

Fig. 1

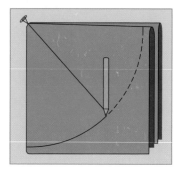

Making Yo-Yo's

To make each yo-yo, cut a circle as indicated in the project instructions. Press the circle edge 1/4" to the wrong side and sew *Running Stitches* (page 139) around the edge with a doubled strand of thread. Pull the thread tightly to gather. Knot and trim the thread ends. Flatten the yo-yo with the small opening at the center of the circle.

Working with Jump Rings

To open a jump ring without putting too much stress on the ring, use 2 pairs of needle-nose jewelry pliers to grasp each side of the ring near the opening. Pull one set of pliers toward you and push the other away to open the ring. Work the pliers in the opposite direction to close the ring.

Embroidery Stitches

BACKSTITCH

Bring the needle up at 1, go down at 2, come up at 3 and go down at 4. Continue working as shown in Fig. 1.

Fig. 1

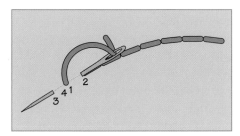

BLANKET STITCH

Referring to Fig. 2, bring the needle up at 1. Keeping the thread below the point of the needle, go down at 2 and come up at 3. Continue working as shown (Fig. 3).

Fig. 2

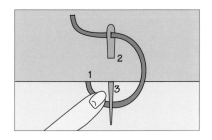

Fig. 3

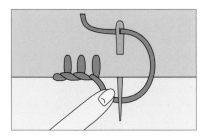

FRENCH KNOT

Referring to Fig. 4, bring the needle up at 1. Wrap the floss once around the needle and insert the needle at 2, holding the floss end with non-stitching fingers. Tighten the knot; then, pull the needle through the fabric, holding the floss until it must be released. For a larger knot, use more strands; wrap only once.

Fig. 4

LAZY DAISY

Bring the needle up at 1; take the needle down at 2 to form a loop and bring the needle up at 3. Keeping the loop below the point of the needle (Fig. 5), take the needle down at 4 to anchor the loop.

Fig. 5

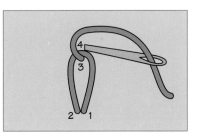

RUNNING STITCH

Referring to Fig. 6, make a series of straight stitches with the stitch length equal to the space between stitches.

Fig. 6

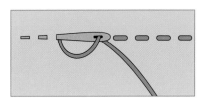

SATIN STITCH

Referring to Fig. 7, come up at odd numbers and go down at even numbers with the stitches touching but not overlapping.

Fig. 7

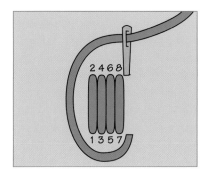

STEM STITCH

Referring to Fig. 8, come up at 1. Keeping the thread below the stitching line, go down at 2 and come up at 3. Go down at 4 and come up at 5.

Fig. 8

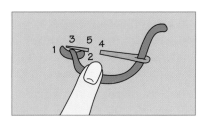

STRAIGHT STITCH

Referring to Fig. 9, come up at 1 and go down at 2.

Fig. 9

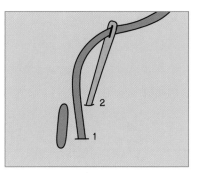

Felted Wool Balls

Pour 6 cups of hot water in a plastic basin; mix in 4 tablespoons of liquid dishwashing detergent. Tear roving into 4" to 5" long sections.

For a foam-based ball, dip a foam ball in the soapy water (wearing rubber gloves if desired). Use dry fingers to tightly wrap a piece of roving around the wet ball. Roll the ball in your hands for a few minutes to help the fibers interlock. Dip the ball in the water again and add more roving, wrapping in a different direction. Repeat until the ball is well covered (some shrinkage will occur as it dries). Allow the ball to dry overnight.

For an all-wool ball, squeeze a fist-sized piece of roving into a tight ball. Dip the ball in the soapy water (wearing rubber gloves if desired) and squeeze several times to shape the ball. Add one new length of dry roving at a time, wrapping in a different direction. Roll the ball in your hands for a few minutes between each added layer to help the fibers interlock. This ball will shrink quite a bit more than a foam-based ball, so make it larger than your desired finished size. Allow the ball to dry overnight.

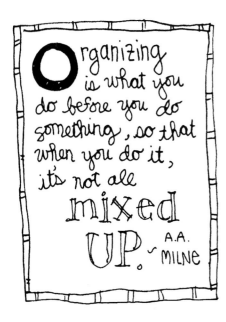

Organizing is what you do before you do something, so that when you do it, it's not all mixed UP. ~A.A. MILNE

Needle Felting

Visit leisurearts.com to view a short needle felting Webcast.

Apply wool felt appliqués, yarn or roving to background fabric using a needle felting tool and mat (Fig. 1). Lightly punch the needles to interlock the fibers and join the pieces without sewing or gluing (Fig. 2). The brush-like mat allows the needles to easily pierce the fibers. We used the Clover Felting Needle Tool to make our projects...it has a locking plastic shield that provides protection from the sharp needles. Felt, wool and woven cotton fabrics all work well as background fabrics.

Fig. 1

Fig. 2

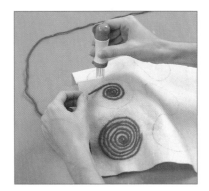

Felting

For the felting process to work, choose an item with wool content of 60% or higher.

1. Set your top-loading washing machine for a HOT wash cycle and a COLD rinse cycle. Add about a tablespoon of laundry detergent.

2. Place the item in a tight-mesh lingerie or sweater bag and toss into the machine. Check every 2-3 minutes during the agitation part of the wash cycle to keep an eye on the amount of felting and the final size. A properly felted item has shrunk to the desired size and the stitches are no longer easy to see. You may want to wear rubber gloves for this, as the water can be very hot.

3. Once the item has felted to your satisfaction, remove it from the washer, spin out the wash water and then run the item through the cold rinse part of the cycle. To avoid setting permanent creases, don't let the item go through the spin portion of the cycle.

4. While wet, shape the item, stretching it to the finished size. Let the item air dry, which may take a day or two depending on the weather.

Pom-Poms

Cut a 4"-long cardboard strip half the diameter of the pom-pom you want to make. Place an 8" piece of yarn along one long edge of the strip. Follow Fig. 1 to wrap yarn around and around the strip and yarn piece (the more you wrap, the fluffier the pom-pom). Tie the wound yarn together tightly with the 8" piece. Leaving the tie ends long to attach the pom-pom, cut the loops opposite the tie; then, fluff and trim the pom-pom into a smooth ball.

Fig. 1

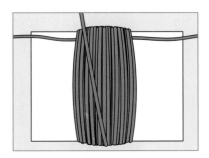

Knit

ABBREVIATIONS

cm	centimeters
K	knit
mm	millimeters
P	purl
PSSO	pass slipped stitch over
st(s)	stitch(es)
tog	together
YO	yarn over

★ — work instructions following ★ as many **more** times as indicated in addition to the first time.

( ) or [ ] — work enclosed instructions **as many** times as specified by the number immediately following **or** work all enclosed instructions in the stitch or space indicated **or** contains explanatory remarks.

colon (:) — the number(s) given after a colon at the end of a row denote(s) the number of stitches you should have on that row.

GAUGE

Exact gauge is **essential** for proper size. Before beginning your project, make the sample swatch given in the individual instructions in the yarn and needle specified. After completing the swatch, measure it, counting your stitches and rows carefully. If your swatch is larger or smaller than specified, make another, changing needle size to get the correct gauge. Keep trying until you find the size needles that will give you the specified gauge.

MARKERS

As a convenience to you, we have used markers to help distinguish a pattern. Place markers as instructed. You may use purchased markers or tie a length of contrasting color yarn around the needle. When you reach a marker on each row, slip it from the left needle to the right needle; remove it when no longer needed.

INCREASE

Knit the next stitch but do **not** slip the old stitch off the left needle (Fig. 1a). Insert the right needle into the **back** loop of the **same** stitch and knit it (Fig. 1b), then slip the old stitch off the left needle.

Fig. 1a

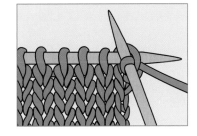

Fig. 1b

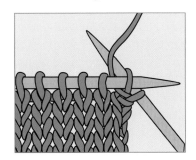

YARN OVERS

After a knit stitch, before a purl stitch

Bring yarn forward **between** the needles, then back **over** the top of the right hand needle and forward **between** the needles again, so that it is now in position to purl the next stitch (Fig. 2a).

Fig. 2a

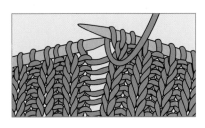

After a purl stitch, before a knit stitch

Take yarn **over** right hand needle to the back, so that it is now in position to knit the next stitch (Fig. 2b).

Fig. 2b

KNIT 2 TOGETHER

(abbreviated K2 tog)

Insert the right needle into the **front** of the first two stitches on the left needle as if to **knit** (Fig. 3); then, **knit** them together as if they were one stitch.

Fig. 3

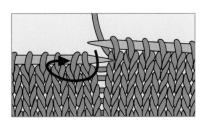

(continued on page 142)

PURL 2 TOGETHER
(abbreviated P2 tog)

Insert the right needle into the **front** of the first two stitches on the left needle as if to **purl** (Fig. 4); then, **purl** them together as if they were one stitch.

Fig. 4

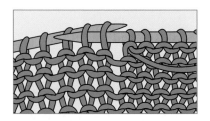

SLIP 1, KNIT 1, PASS SLIPPED STITCH OVER
(abbreviated slip 1, K1, PSSO)

Slip one stitch as if to **knit** (Fig. 5a). Knit the next stitch. With the left needle, bring the slipped stitch over the knit stitch (Fig. 5b) and off the needle.

Fig. 5a

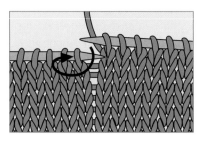

Fig. 5b

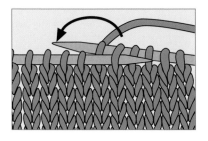

PICKING UP STITCHES

When instructed to pick up stitches, insert the needle from the **front** to the **back** under two strands at the edge of the worked piece (Fig. 6). Put the yarn around the needle as if to **knit**; then, bring the needle with the yarn back through the stitch to the right side, resulting in a stitch on the needle. Repeat this along the edge, picking up the required number of stitches. A crochet hook may be helpful to pull the yarn through.

Fig. 6

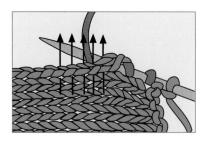

WEAVING SEAMS

With the **right** side of both pieces facing you and edges even, sew through both sides once to secure the seam. Insert the needle under the bar **between** the first and second stitches on the row and pull the yarn through (Fig. 7). Insert the needle under the next bar on the second side. Repeat from side to side, being careful to match rows. If the edges are different lengths, it may be necessary to insert the needle under two bars at one edge.

Fig. 7

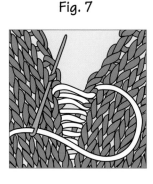

Crochet
ABBREVIATIONS

ch(s)	chain(s)
cm	centimeters
dc	double crochet(s)
FP	Front Post
FPdc	Front Post double crochet(s)
mm	millimeters
Rnd(s)	Round(s)
sc	single crochet(s)
sp(s)	space(s)
st(s)	stitch(es)
YO	yarn over

★ — work instructions following ★ as many **more** times as indicated in addition to the first time.

† to † — work all instructions from first † to second † **as many** times as specified.

( ) or [ ] — work enclosed instructions **as many** times as specified by the number immediately following **or** work all enclosed instructions in the stitch or space indicated **or** contains explanatory remarks.

colon (:) — the number(s) given after a colon at the end of a row or round denote(s) the number of stitches you should have on that row or round.

GAUGE

Exact gauge is **essential** for proper size. Before beginning your project, make the sample swatch given in the individual instructions in the yarn and hook specified. After completing the swatch, measure it, counting your stitches and rows or rounds carefully. If your swatch is larger or smaller than specified, make another, changing hook size to get the correct gauge. Keep trying until you find the size hook that will give you the specified gauge.

MARKERS

Markers are used to help distinguish the beginning of each round being worked. Place a 2" (5 cm) scrap piece of yarn before the first stitch of each round, moving marker after each round is complete.

JOINING WITH Sc

When instructed to join with sc, begin with a slip knot on the hook. Insert the hook in the stitch or space indicated, YO and pull up a loop, YO and draw through both loops on the hook.

BACK RIDGE

Work only in loops indicated by arrows (Fig. 1).

Fig. 1

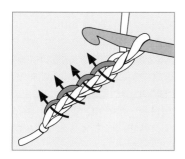

FREE LOOPS OF BEGINNING CHAIN

When instructed to work in free loops of a chain, work in loop indicated by arrow (Fig. 2).

Fig. 2

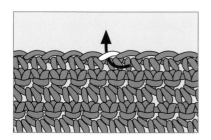

FRONT POST STITCH

Work around post of stitch indicated, inserting hook in direction of arrow (Fig. 3).

Fig. 3

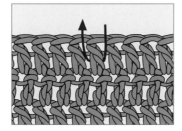

REVERSE SINGLE CROCHET
(abbreviated reverse sc)

Working from left to **right**, ★ insert hook in st to **right** of hook (Fig. 4a), YO and draw through, under and to left of loop on hook (2 loops on hook) (Fig. 4b), YO and draw through both loops on hook (Fig. 4c) **(reverse sc made, Fig. 4d)**; repeat from ★ around.

Fig. 4a

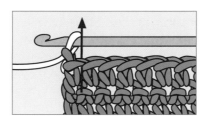

Fig. 4b

Fig. 4c

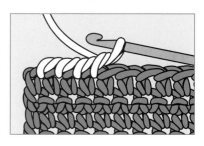

Fig. 4d

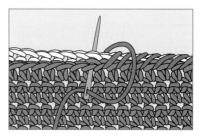

WHIPSTITCH

Place two Strips with **wrong** sides together. Sew through both pieces once to secure the beginning of the seam, leaving an ample yarn end to weave in later. Insert the needle from **front** to **back** through **both** loops on **both** pieces (Fig. 5). Bring the needle around and insert it from **front** to **back** through next loops of both pieces. Continue in this manner across, keeping the sewing yarn fairly loose.

Fig. 5

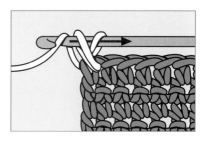

GOING HOME FOR THE HOLIDAYS IS GOOD FOR THE HEART ★ SURPRISE SOMEBODY SPECIAL!

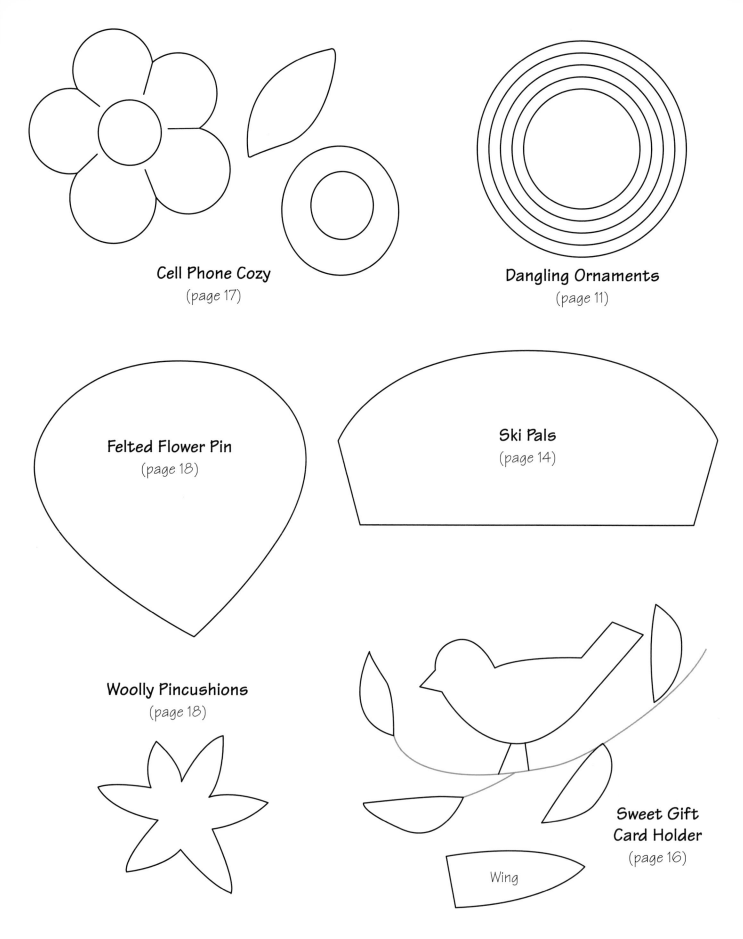

Cell Phone Cozy
(page 17)

Dangling Ornaments
(page 11)

Felted Flower Pin
(page 18)

Ski Pals
(page 14)

Woolly Pincushions
(page 18)

Sweet Gift
Card Holder
(page 16)

Wing

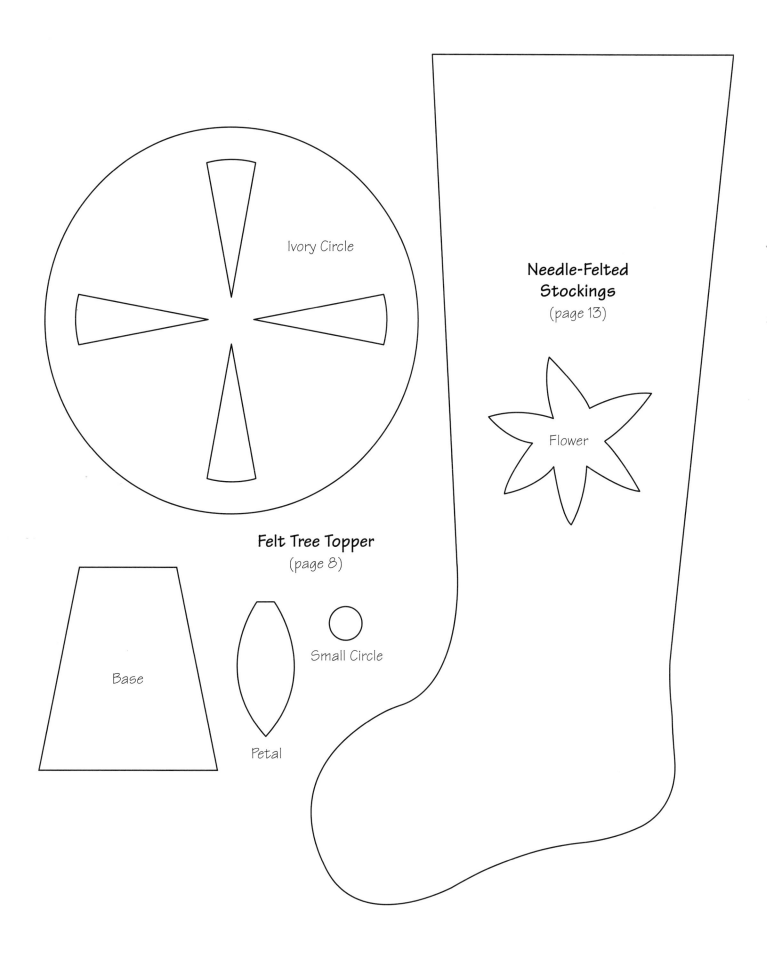

Ivory Circle

Needle-Felted
Stockings
(page 13)

Flower

Felt Tree Topper
(page 8)

Small Circle

Base

Petal

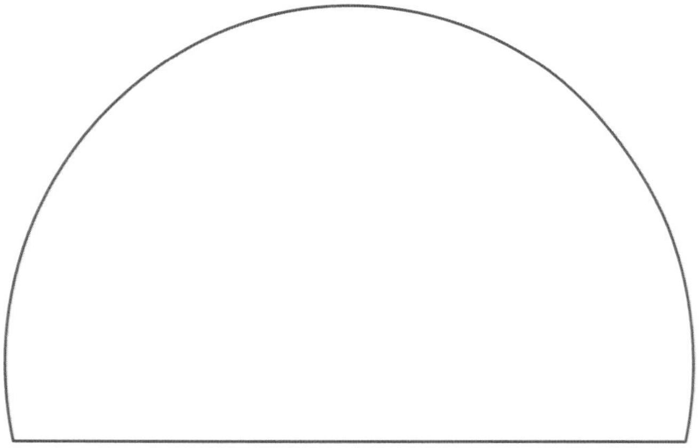

Needle-Felted Tree Skirt

(page 10)

Round Flower
Flower Centers

KEY

• French Knot

Lazy Daisy

Fanciful Journal Cover

(page 16)

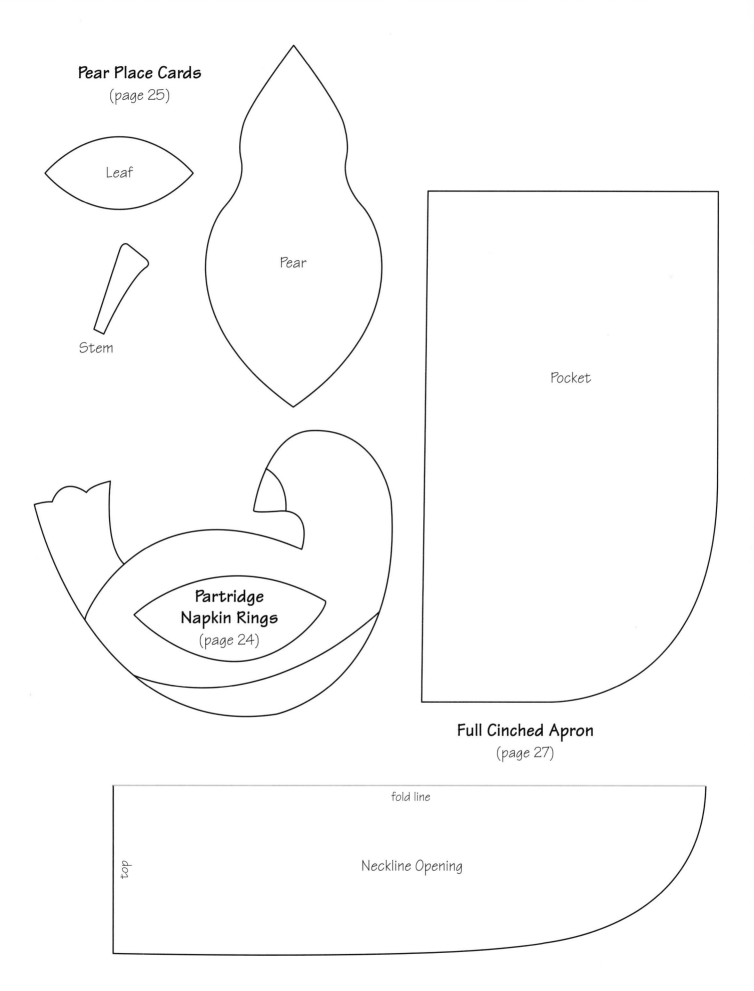

Pear Place Cards
(page 25)

Leaf

Stem

Pear

Pocket

Partridge Napkin Rings
(page 24)

Full Cinched Apron
(page 27)

fold line

top

Neckline Opening

147

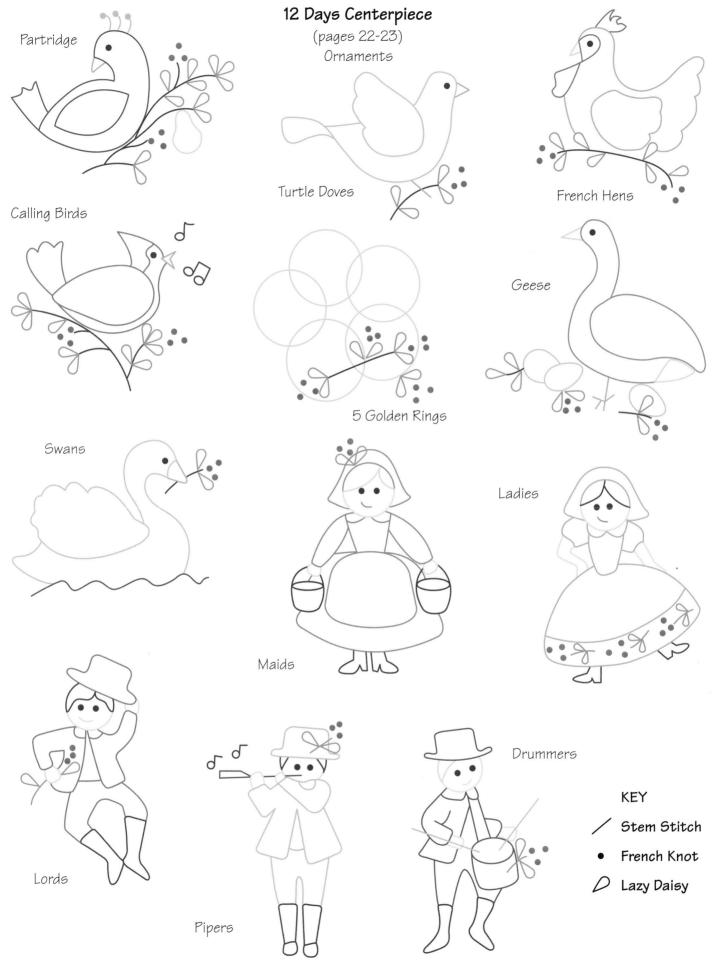

Partridge

12 Days Centerpiece
(pages 22-23)
Ornaments

Turtle Doves

French Hens

Calling Birds

5 Golden Rings

Geese

Swans

Ladies

Maids

Lords

Drummers

Pipers

KEY

╱ Stem Stitch

● French Knot

◠ Lazy Daisy

148

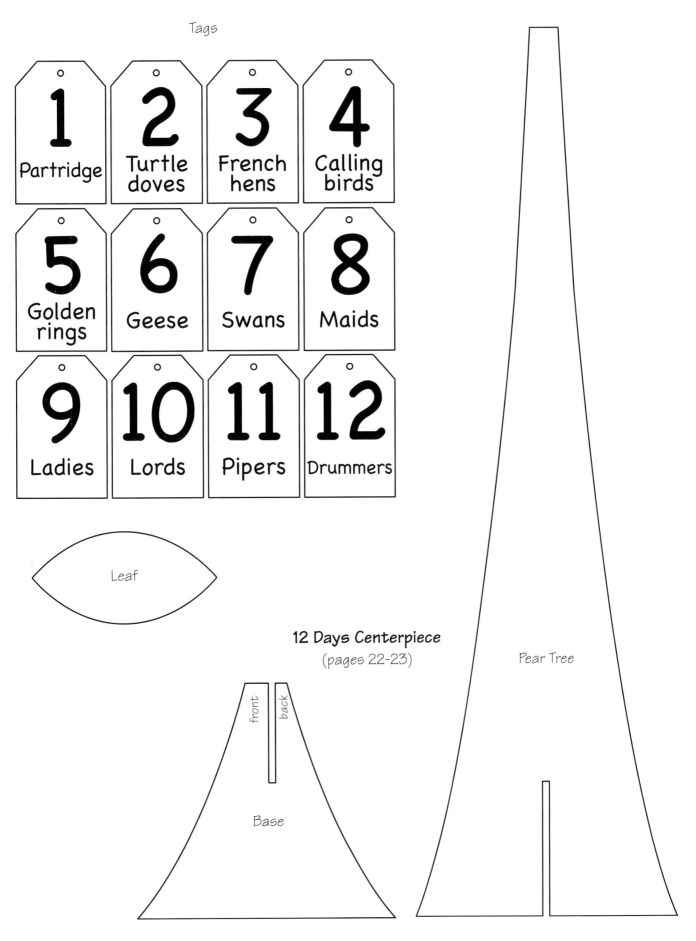

Tags

1 Partridge
2 Turtle doves
3 French hens
4 Calling birds
5 Golden rings
6 Geese
7 Swans
8 Maids
9 Ladies
10 Lords
11 Pipers
12 Drummers

Leaf

12 Days Centerpiece
(pages 22-23)

front
back

Base

Pear Tree

149

Inviting Bench
(page 37)

Woodsy Welcome
(page 30)

Mitten Insert

Skate Insert

Knit Skate Ornament
(page 40)

Knit Mitten (Ornament)
(page 40)

Skate Blade

Ice Skating Scene

(page 41)

Background Trees A

Cottage Tree A

Cottage Tree B

Background Trees B

Foreground Trees A

Foreground Tree B

Skaters

Paper Snowflakes

(page 34)

JOY Banner
(page 47)

Snowbound Tray
(page 53)

KEY

— — — Running Stitch

- - - - - Backstitch

/// Straight Stitch

——— Stem Stitch

⟋ Lazy Daisy

• • French Knot

Redbird Collage Card
(page 57)

Felt Fob
(page 52)

KEY

// Stem Stitch

ꝺꝺꝺ Lazy Daisy

Posy Pendant
(page 50)

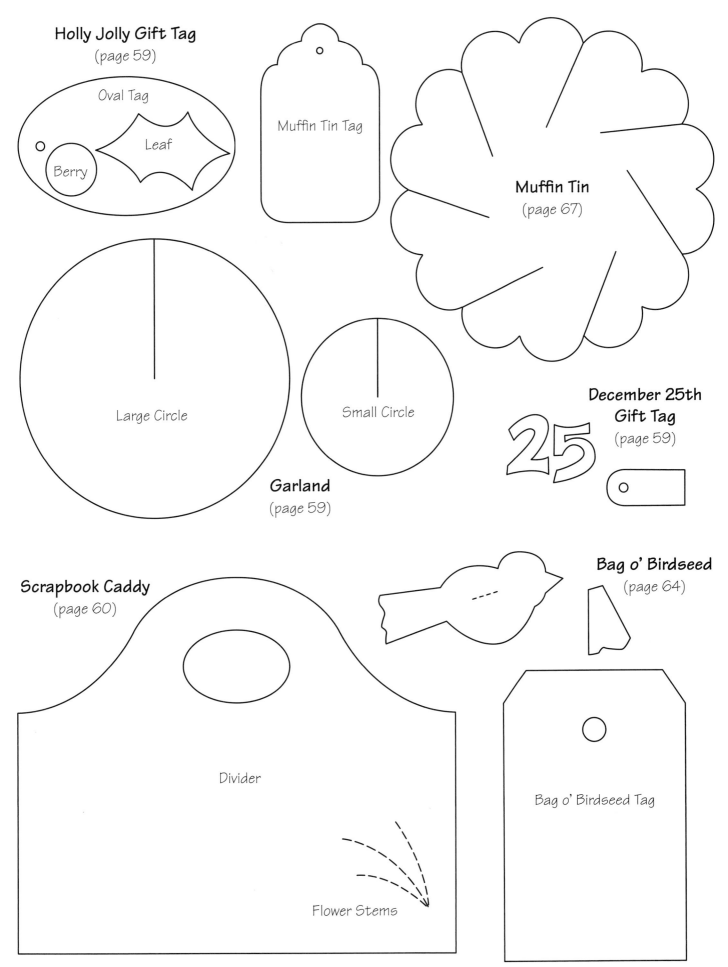

Holly Jolly Gift Tag

(page 59)

Oval Tag

Leaf

Berry

Muffin Tin Tag

Muffin Tin

(page 67)

Large Circle

Small Circle

December 25th Gift Tag

(page 59)

25

Garland

(page 59)

Bag o' Birdseed

(page 64)

Scrapbook Caddy

(page 60)

Divider

Flower Stems

Bag o' Birdseed Tag

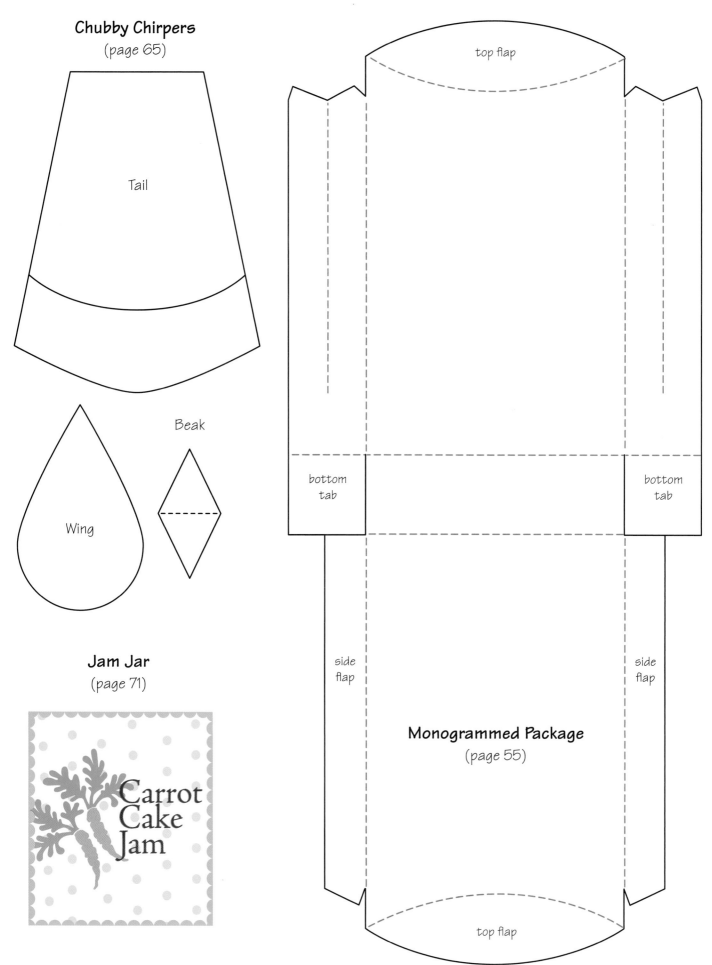

Chubby Chirpers
(page 65)

Tail

Beak

Wing

Jam Jar
(page 71)

Carrot Cake Jam

Monogrammed Package
(page 55)

top flap

bottom tab

bottom tab

side flap

side flap

top flap

154

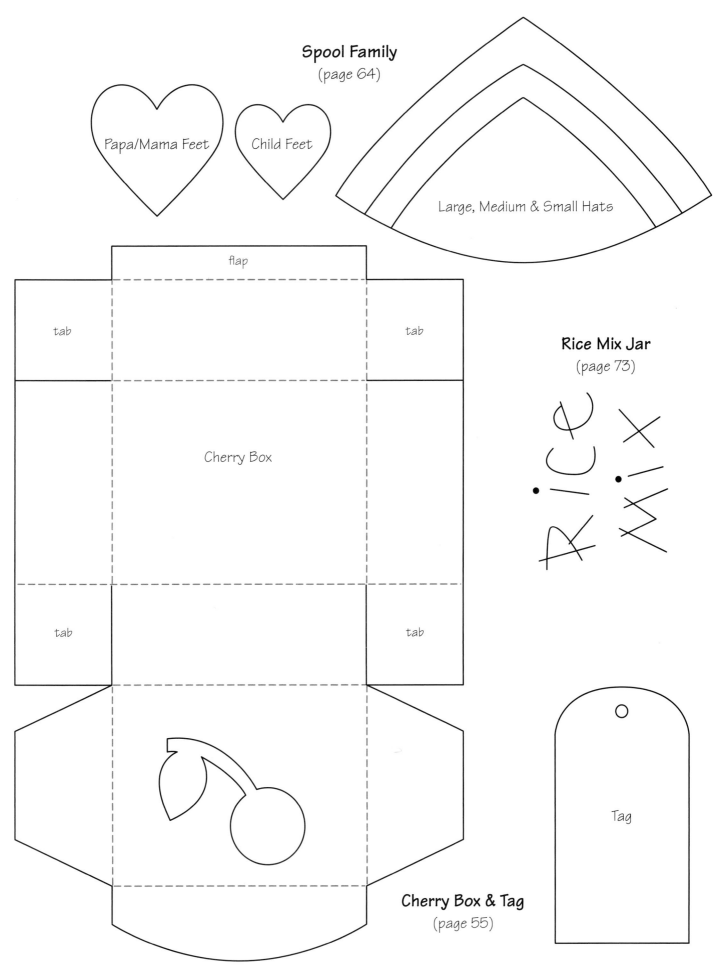

Spool Family
(page 64)

Papa/Mama Feet

Child Feet

Large, Medium & Small Hats

flap

tab

tab

Rice Mix Jar
(page 73)

Rice Mix

tab

tab

Cherry Box

Tag

Cherry Box & Tag
(page 55)

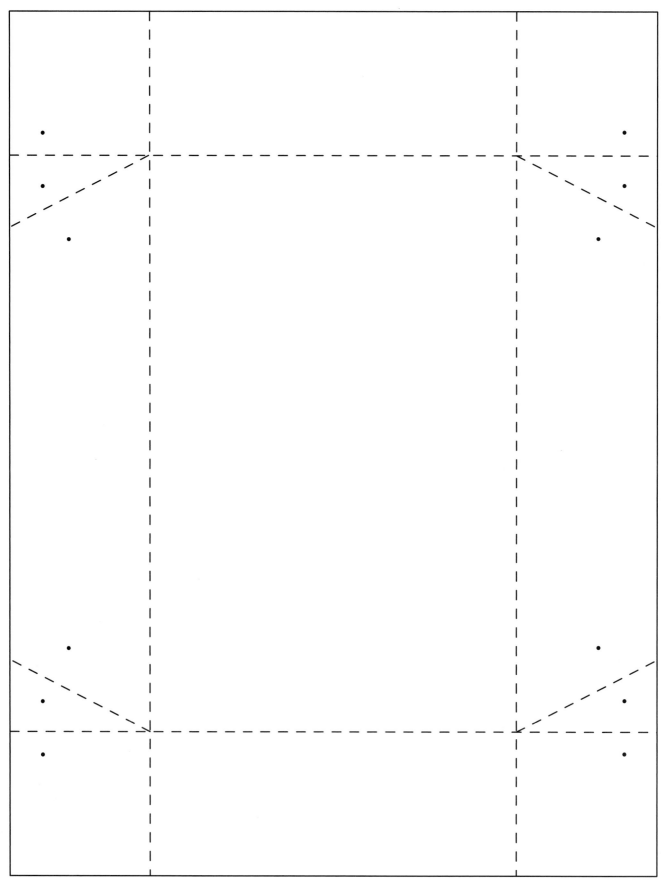

Paper Trays

(page 75)

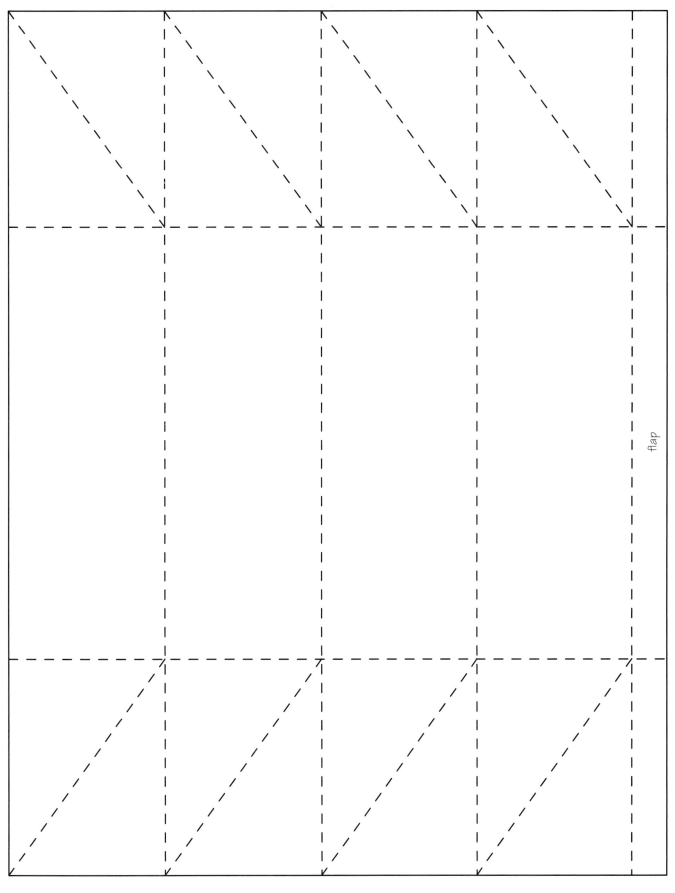

flap

Fudge Box

(page 68)

Project Index

Recipe Index

Credits

We want to extend a warm "Thank you!" to the people who allowed us to photograph some of our projects at their homes: Desmond & Carol Doris, Justin & Jennie Jaksha, Bill & Lynn Phelps, Scott & Angela Simon and Ron & Becky Werle.

We want to especially thank Mark Mathews of Mark Mathews Photography for his excellent work.

We would like to recognize the following companies for providing some of the materials and tools we used to make our projects: Colonial Needle, Inc. (colonialneedle.com) for the wool roving; Clover Needlecraft, Inc. (clover-usa.com) for the felting needle tool and mat; Patons® (patonsyarns.com) and Lion Brand® Yarn (lionbrand.com) for yarn; The DMC Corporation (dmc-usa.com) for embroidery floss; National Nonwovens (nationalnonwovens.com) for wool felt and Saral® Paper Corporation (saralpaper.com) for transfer paper.

Special thanks to JoAnn Bowling, Marianna Crowder, Sue Galucki and Freda Gillham for knitting and crocheting some of our photo models.

A very special thank you to Kay Meadors for designing the Flap Cap, to Brenda E. Stratton of Alexander-Stratton Designs, Inc. for the Woodland Throw and to Arleen Wurman for the Knit Tree Skirt.

If these cozy Christmas ideas have inspired you to look for more Gooseberry Patch® publications, find us online at www.gooseberrypatch.com and see what's new. We're on Facebook and Twitter too, so you can keep up with us even more often!